AF512984

Artificial Intelligence

Textbook

5

Harmeet Kaur
M. Anhitha

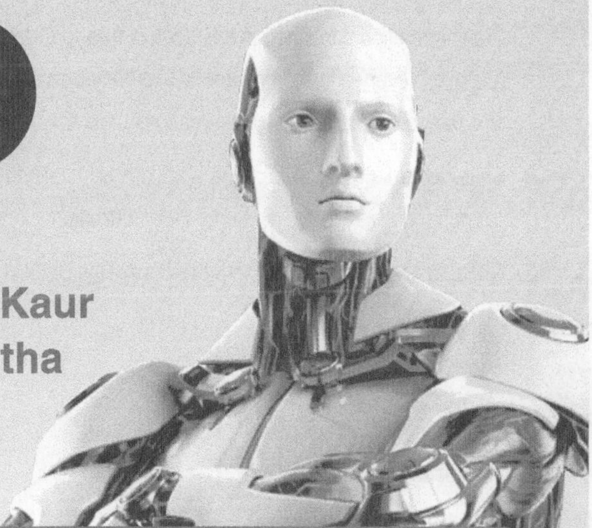

Name ....

Class .... **Section** .... **Roll No** ....

School ....

Address ....

Phone ....

bpb
www.bpbonline.com

FIRST EDITION 2021

ISBN: 978-93-90684-861

Distributors:

BPB PUBLICATIONS

20, Ansari Road, Darya Ganj

New Delhi-110002

Ph: 23254990/23254991

DECCAN AGENCIES

4-3-329, Bank Street,

Hyderabad-500195

Ph: 24756967/24756400

MICRO MEDIA

Shop No. 5, Mahendra Chambers,

150 DN Rd. Next to Capital Cinema,

V.T. (C.S.T.) Station, MUMBAI-400 001

Ph: 22078296/22078297

BPB BOOK CENTRE

376 Old Lajpat Rai Market,

Delhi-110006

Ph: 23861747

To View Complete
BPB Publications Catalogue
Scan the QR Code:

Published by Manish Jain for BPB Publications, 20 Ansari Road, Darya Ganj, New Delhi-110002 and Printed at Manipal Technologies Ltd., Karnataka (India)

www.bpbonline.com

Dedicated to

Our parents, family members, peers & dear students.

About the Authors

Harmeet Kaur is currently working as Senior Computer Teacher, Department of Computer Science at Heritage Xperiential Learning School, Gurugram. She has over 23 years of experience in the field of education; teaching Computer Science, Informatics Practices and Multimedia and Web Technologies to grades XI and XII along with a background of mentoring, IT curriculum development for STEM integration, and staff training and development. She has led various in-house projects such as Learning Management System to propagate collaborative personalized e-Learning. She is well adept in Google Apps for Education and uses it as a primary platform for her classroom teaching. She integrates multiple teaching styles to build digital literacy skills in millennial learners while strongly promoting safe and ethical use of technology. She believes in driving the experiential and project-based pedagogy by imparting mobile computing skills to high school students. She has conducted various workshops in and around Delhi-NCR to train teachers with latest pedagogies of classroom management, incorporating Tech to teach STEM education and "learning by doing" hands-on workshops. She has authored training material for in-house teacher training and been constructive in ICT curriculum development.

LinkedIn: linkedin.com/in/harmeetkaur2504

Website: www.harmeetkaur.in

M. Anhitha has an overall professional experience of more than 9 years. She has written many books including Fundamentals of computer science, Information Technology and currently working as a writer in computer science where she collaborates and works with enthusiasts across the globe. She has done B.Tech in Information Technology and M.Tech in Computer Science. She likes to keep herself updated to the latest trends and technologies.

LinkedIn: linkedin.com/in/m-anhitha-234130206

Blog: https://taartech.blogspot.com/

Acknowledgements

We would like to express our gratitude to everyone at BPB Publications for giving us this opportunity to write the book. We are thankful to all the resource persons at BPB Publications for editing, technical reviewing and language editing the book.

We are thankful to each other and our families for being supportive in numerous ways and for giving their unconditional love and support at all times.

Lastly, but not the least, we would like to thank God for bearing us with courage and humility to be able to write this book for our students.

— Harmeet Kaur

— M. Anhitha

Preface

Artificial Intelligence is the driving force which shall pave the path of success for the future generations. Selfdriving cars, Automated task, Robotic gadgets; are becoming an integral part of our everyday lives. When someone mentions the word "AI"; the first thing that comes to our mind is a visual of a Robot which is capable of doing amazing things which humans cannot do.

The book is divided into three chapters and provides a detailed description of the basic concept of Artificial Intelligence.

Chapter 1 excites the learner to explore and get motivated about Artificial Intelligence applications in daily life. The chapter entails multiple gaming activities to make them understand the applications, advantages, disadvantages of AI, Machine learning, Data Science, Robotics. The chapter clearly explains the rules for all gaming activities with individualistic learning being encouraged while practicing critical thinking skills.

Chapter 2 contains web accessible resources for the learner to understand the concept of Search and Problem solving with AI. They are able to foresee their expectations for future AI readiness and devise plans with the information collected. The chapter ends with the explanation of Odds and Probability, Bayes rule.

Chapter 3 clearly earmarks the meaning of Machine Learning, Neural Network, Predicting the future and the social implications of AI. The learner is able to determine why machine learning techniques are used and what is AI Ethics?

Each chapter consists of Activities for Interactive Learning, Check Your Progress, Brain Bot, Worksheet, Quiz Card to learn and practice. All the answers are given at the end of the book to test your knowledge.

Throughout the book many activities have been given in the chapter to understand the concept in a better way.

Sample project has been given which explains the interface of Scratch and then teaches you to create a very interesting project of "**Zombie Escape**".

To practice and to get the idea of the exam pattern, one Sample Paper has been given to practice.

Key terms in the form of glossary have been given to enhance the learning.

Contents

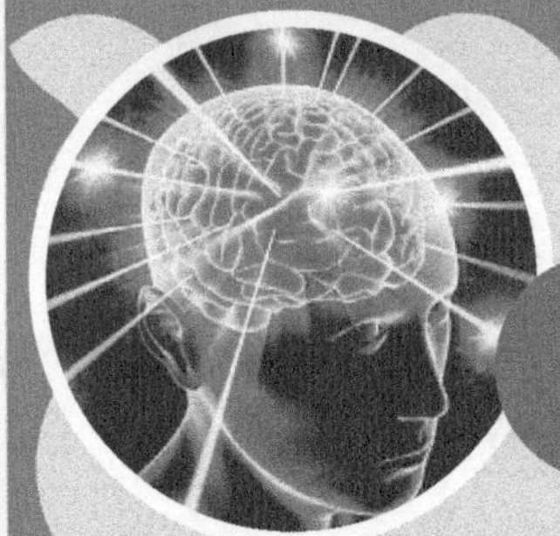

1 INTRODUCTION TO ARTIFICIAL INTELLIGENCE

Structure Bot

In this chapter, we will discuss:

- The meaning of the term Artificial Intelligence
- Applications, Advantages and Disadvantages of Artificial Intelligence
- Domains of Artificial Intelligence

Objective Bot

At the end of this chapter, you should be able to:

- Know the use of AI in various applications
- Learn about Machine Learning, Data Science
- Understand the meaning and applications of Robots

Introduction to Artificial Intelligence

Artificial intelligence (AI) is an intelligence which is demonstrated by machines.

A quip in Tesler's Theorem says "*AI is whatever hasn't been done yet.*"

AI is an artificial life-forms which surpass human intelligence, or it may be a data processing technology. You can see AI in:

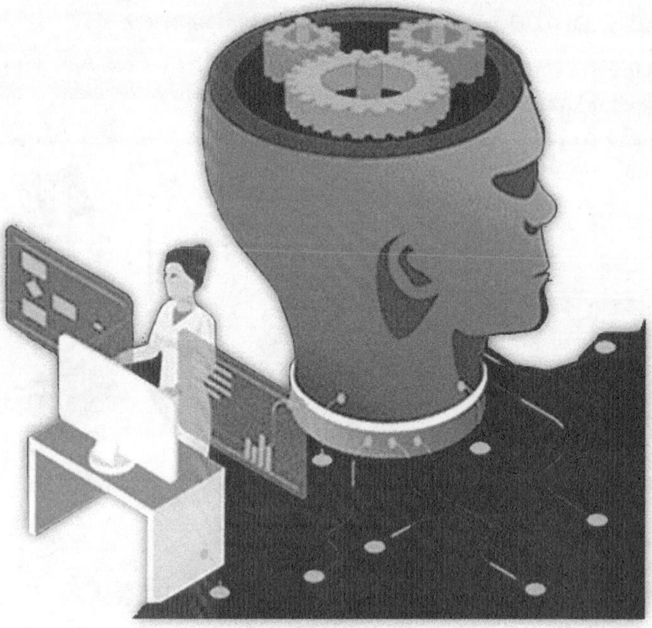

Self-driving cars:

(Vehicle capable of sensing environment and moving safely with no or little human input)

- It works on combination of AI technique:
  - **Search and planning** to find out the most convenient route from one point to another.
  - **Computer vision** to identify obstacles.
  - **Decision making** under uncertainty to cope with the complex and dynamic environment.

Content recommendation

(Content of your interest)

- Facebook, Twitter, Instagram, and other social media content.
- Music recommendations on Spotify.
- Movie recommendations on Netflix, HBO, and other streaming services.

Image and video processing

AI is used to generate or alter visual content. With AI you can make your personal photos to look like they were painted by Vincent van Gogh, and can generated characters in motion pictures such as Avatar, the Lord of the Rings.

Fact Bot

AI is "cool things that computers can't do."

Activity I

Teachable Machine

Description

In this, you will train a computer to recognize your images, sounds, & poses. It's a fast and an easy way to create machine learning models.

To perform an activity:

1. Go to the link: https://teachablemachine.withgoogle.com/
2. The following screen appear:

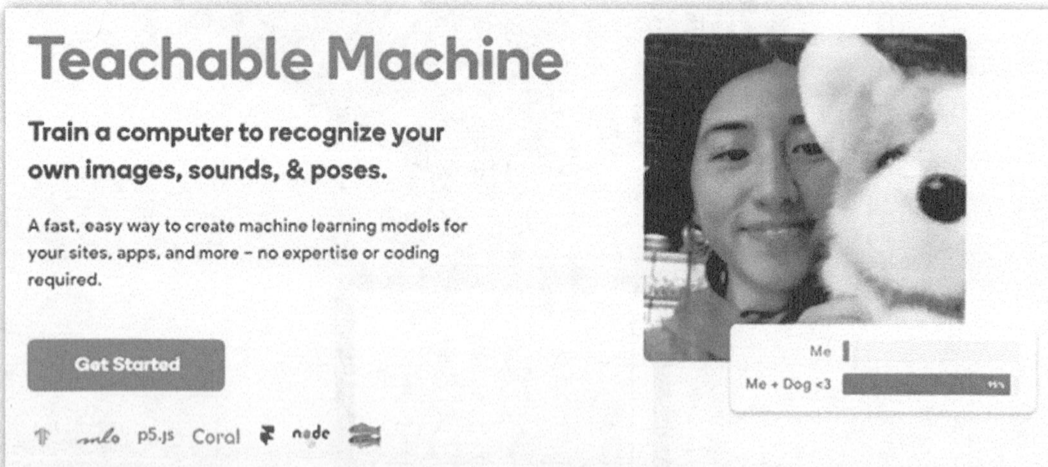

3. Click on Get Started.
4. Next screen as shown appears, click on Image Project.

5. Upload the images in Class 1 and Class 2.

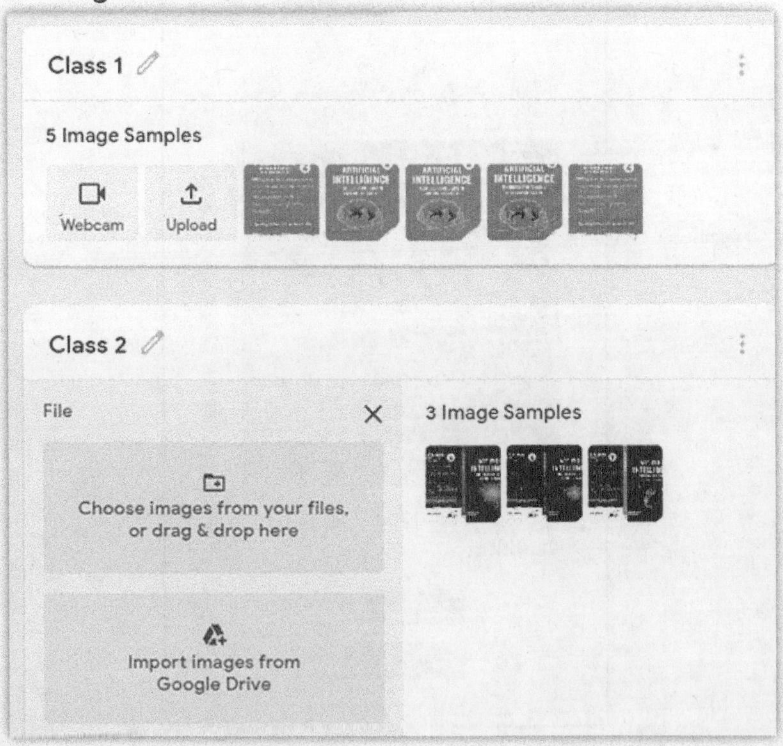

6. Click on the Train Model.

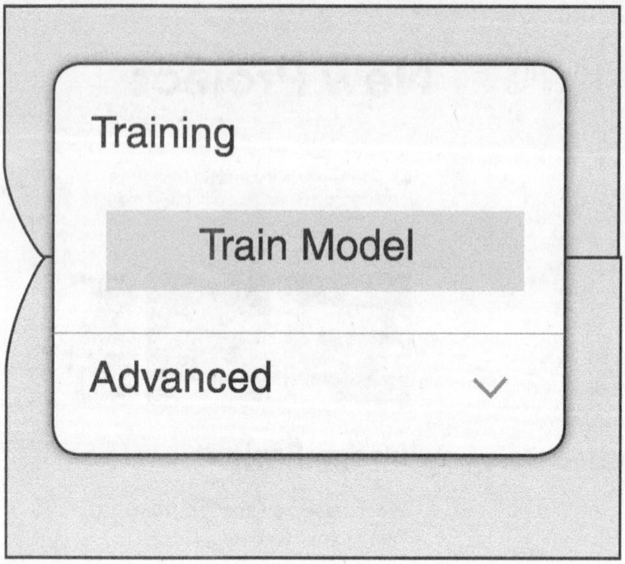

7. Click on Export model. To export the model and use it in your project.

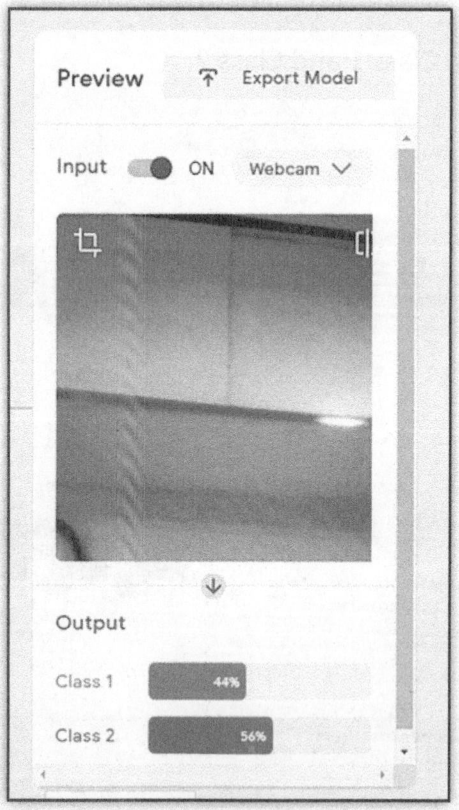

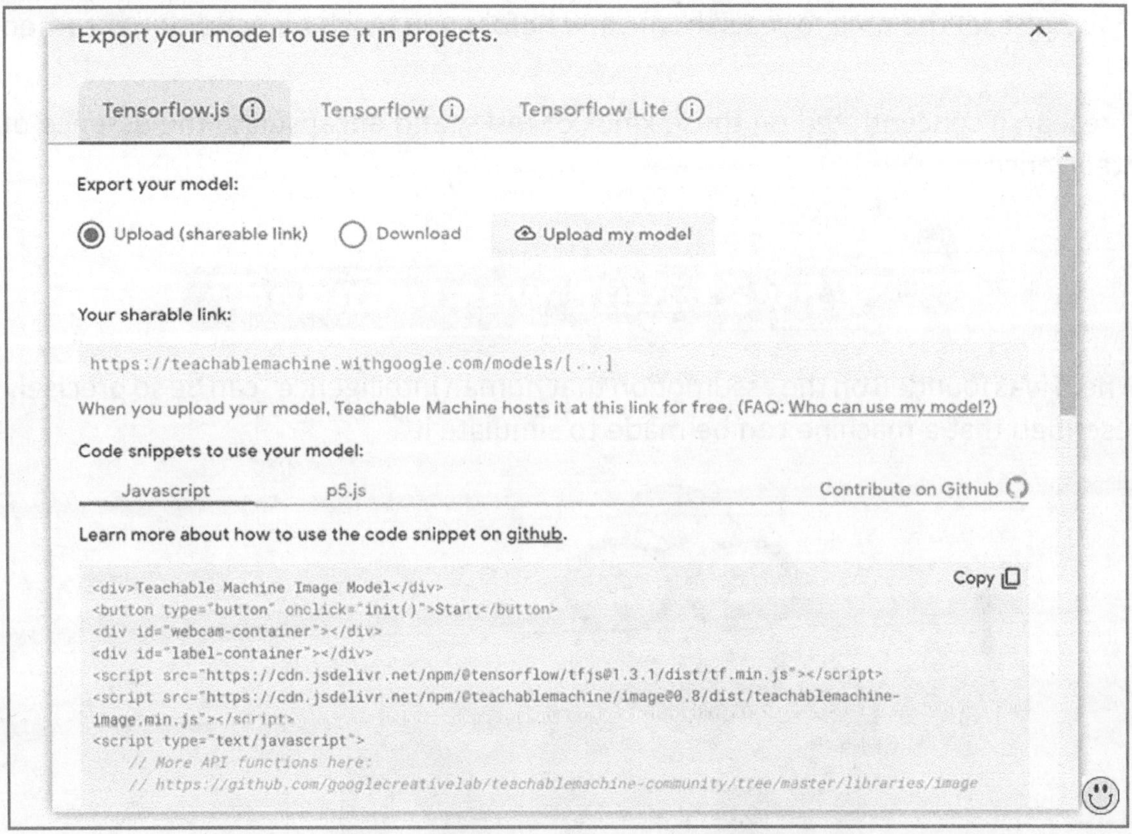

What is, and What isn't AI?

The popularity of AI in the media is because people have started using the term AI when they refer to things which are called by other names.

The field is constantly getting redefined when some topics emerge. **Automatic methods** for search and planning were considered to belong to the domain of AI.

Science fiction stories often feature friendly humanoid servants are the things that AI provide us. With AI, task are getting automated, imagine you are entering into a room and its door get open automatically, or you just set the time to reach home and before you reach Air conditioner turned ON.

AI research concentrated on these kinds of tasks, and encapsulate the essence of intelligence.

Why AI field was founded?

AI field was founded on the assumption that human intelligence "can be so precisely described that a machine can be made to simulate it".

What is Artificial Intelligence?

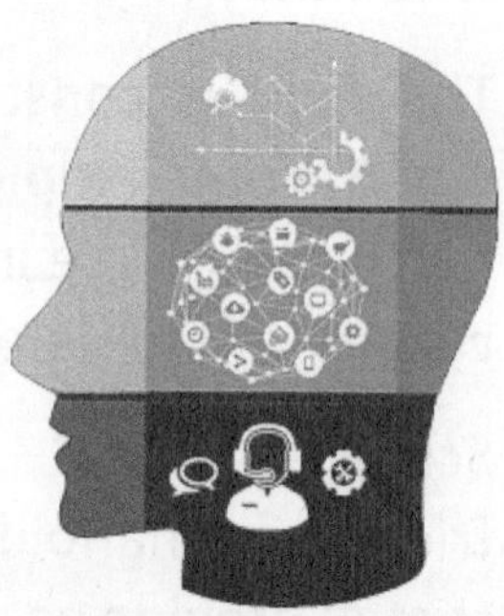

Artificial Intelligence (AI) was first coined in 1956 at Dartmouth Conference by a cognitive scientist, John McCarthy, at the Dartmouth Conference.

Artificial intelligence (AI) refers to the simulation of human intelligence in the machines which are programmed to think like humans and mimic the actions of humans.

DEFINITION

Artificial intelligence is simulation of human intelligence in the machines.

Activity II

Magic SketchPad

Description

In this, you will draw the object along with machine. You will be notify the object to draw and when you lift up the pen in between; a machine learning algorithm will try to finish the left stoke and tries to draw the object which match with the category you have selected.

To perform an activity:

1. Visit the link: https://magic-sketchpad.glitch.me/
2. The following screen appear:

3. Click on LET'S GO!
4. Screen as shown appears:

5. On the top right, you can see the name of the object to be drawn alarm_clock, along with it the save option and help button is present.

   In case if you want to roll back the previous move, click on , and in case to delete the drawing click on .

6. Now start drawing the alarm clock, and where you up the mouse, the rest of the drawing will get completed automatically.

Applications of AI

Marketing: Finding the movies on Netflix.

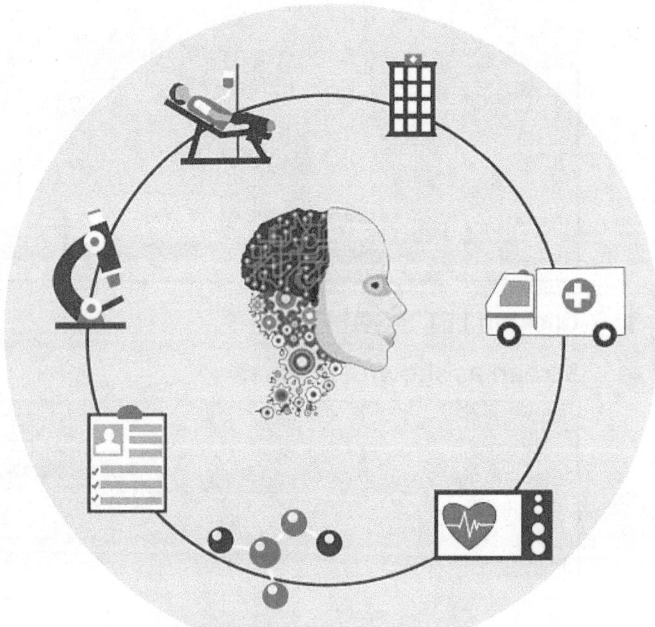

Health Care: When it comes to saving our lives, a lot of organizations and medical care centres are relying on AI.

Tip Bot

Machine learning is the systems that improve the performance in a given task with more and more experience or data.

Agriculture: Approaches to improve crop yield.

Space Exploration: To identify a distant eight-planet solar system.

Chatbots: Virtual assistants to control the appliances at home.

Social Media: For face verification.

Activity III

Blocky Game

Description

Its a block based web browser application, in which you can drag the blocks and keep them together.

To perform an activity:

1. Visit the link: https://blockly.games

2. The following screen appear:

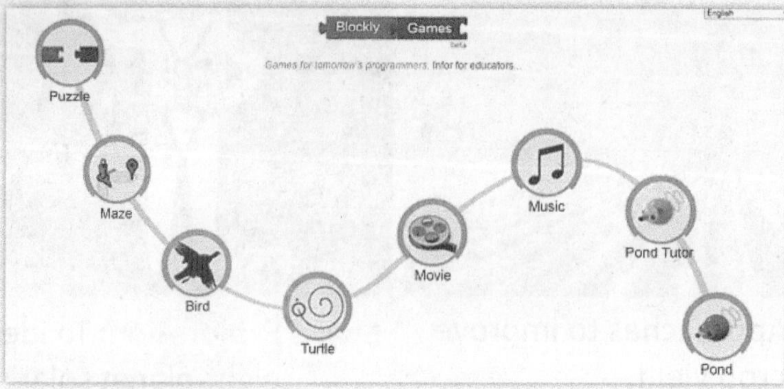

3. Click on Turtle Button.
4. The following screen appears:

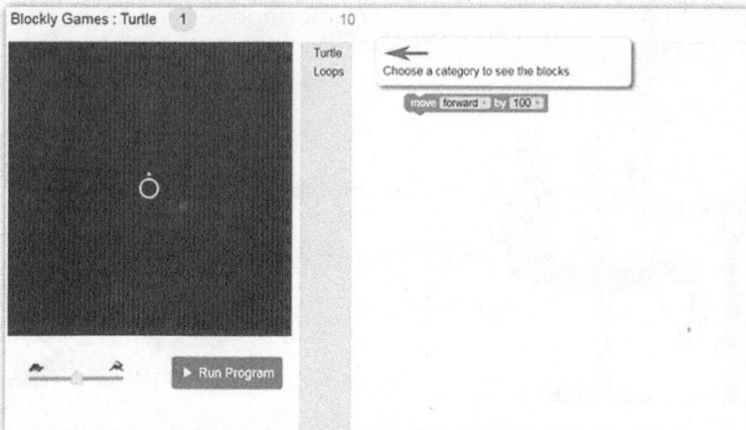

5. Now you have to drag the blocks (By clicking on Turtle) and change it to forward, backward or can turn it to right or left to desired direction to move the turtle to the path as shown in the black screen.
6. Drag the block as shown: (We will be drawing a square of side 100)

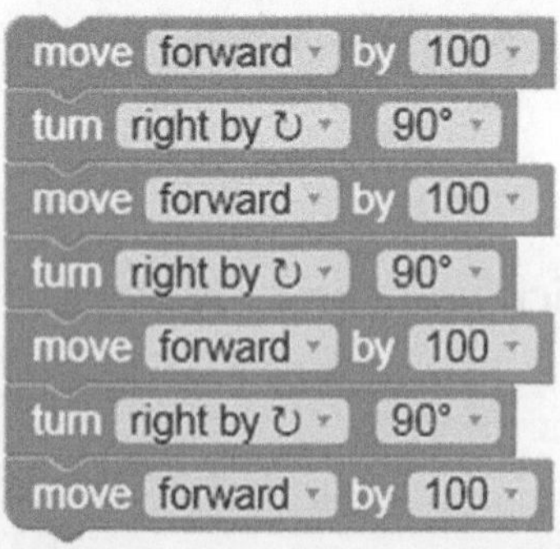

7. Click on Run Program.
8. You can see the turtle moves as per the instruction.

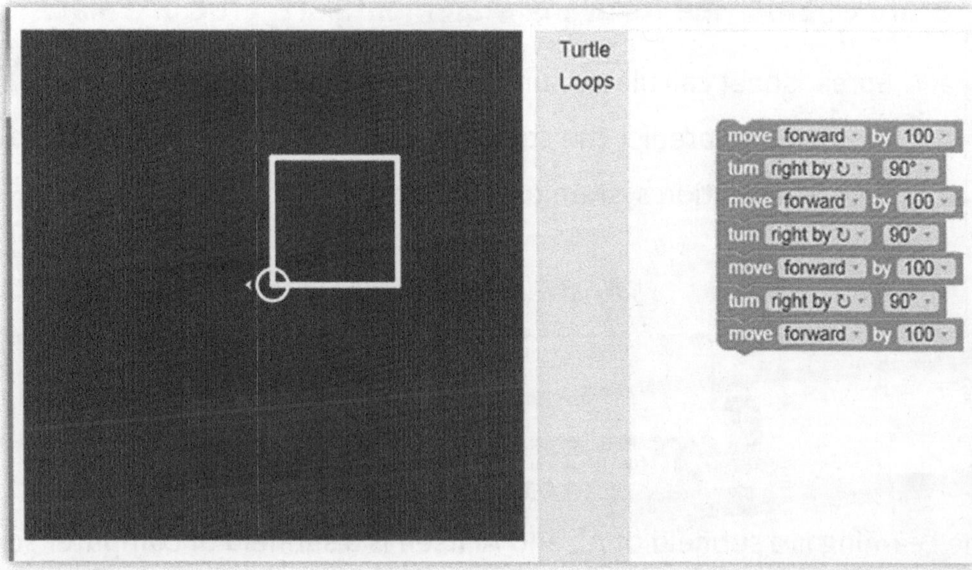

Advantages and Disadvantages of Artificial Intelligence

Advantages	Disadvantages
Reduction in Human Error	High Costs of Creation
Takes risks instead of Humans	Making Humans Lazy
Available 24x7	Unemployment
Helping in Repetitive Jobs	No Emotions

MEMORY BOT

Other than AI, there are many other closely related topics which include Machine Learning, Data Science and Deep Learning.

Check your Progress - I

State whether the following statements are True or False.

a Spreadsheet calculates sum with the help of AI. True / False

b AI is used to predict the stock market. True / False

c A GPS navigation system uses AI for finding the fastest route. True / False

Answer: False, True, True

Machine Learning

Machine Learning is a subfield of AI, and AI itself is a subfield of computer science. Machine learning enables systems to improve their performance in a given task with more and more experience or data.

DEFINITION

Machine learning enables systems to improve its performance in a given task with more and more experience or data.

Applications of Machine Learning

- **Speech Recognition:** While using Google, you get an option of "Search by voice," it comes under speech recognition. It converts voice instructions into text.

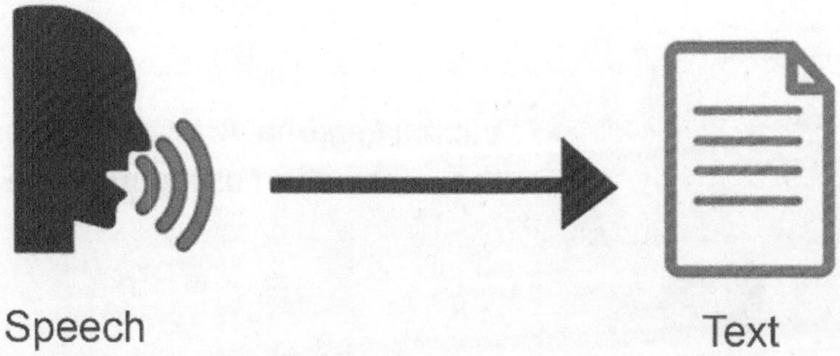

- **Traffic prediction:** Predicting the traffic conditions such as whether traffic is cleared, slow-moving, or heavily congested.

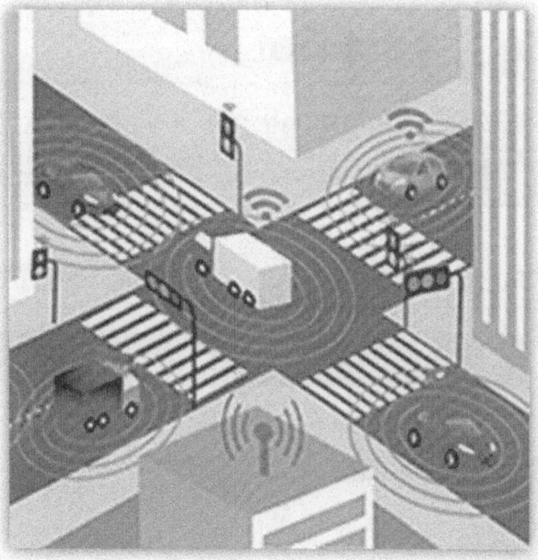

Tip Bot

Machine Learning train the model created from patterns in your data.

- **Product recommendations:** It understands the user interest and suggests the product as per customer interest.

- **Email Spam and Malware Filtering:** New received email, is filtered automatically as important, normal, and spam.

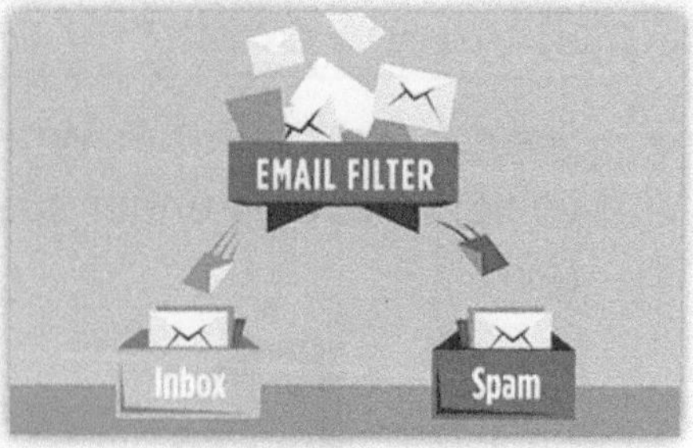

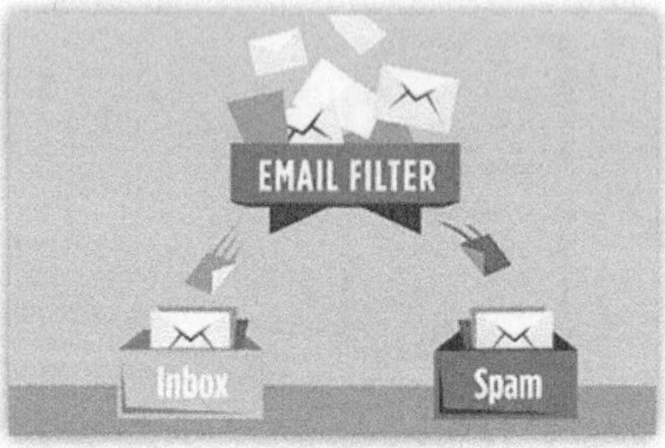

- **Virtual Personal Assistant:** Helps you in finding the information using our voice instruction.

Fact Bot

Machine Learning is a part of Artificial Intelligence which learns from the data and provide results on the basis of analysis.

Advantages and Disadvantages of Machine Learning

Advantages	Disadvantages
Review large volumes of data and discover specific trends and patterns.	Requires massive data sets to train on.
Have the ability to learn, make predictions and improve the algorithms on their own.	Needs enough time to let the algorithms learn and develop enough to fulfill their purpose with accuracy and relevancy.
It keeps improving in accuracy and efficiency on its own.	It is autonomous but highly susceptible to errors.
Handle multi-dimensional and multi-variety data.	More Technical Security Threats.

MEMORY BOT

Machine learning is all about Algorithms and Data.

Activity IV

Blocky Game-II

Description

In Activity III, you have moved the turtle using move and turn block. In this you will learn to move the turtle on the same path by using loops.

To perform an activity:

1. Visit the link: https://blockly.games
2. The following screen appear:

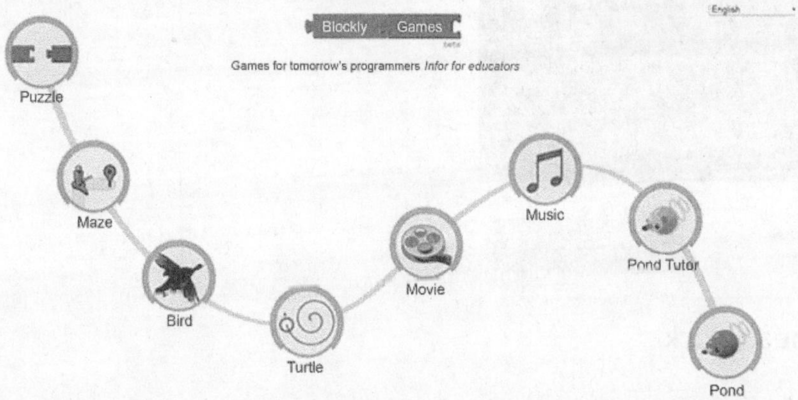

3. Click on Turtle Button.
4. The following screen appears:

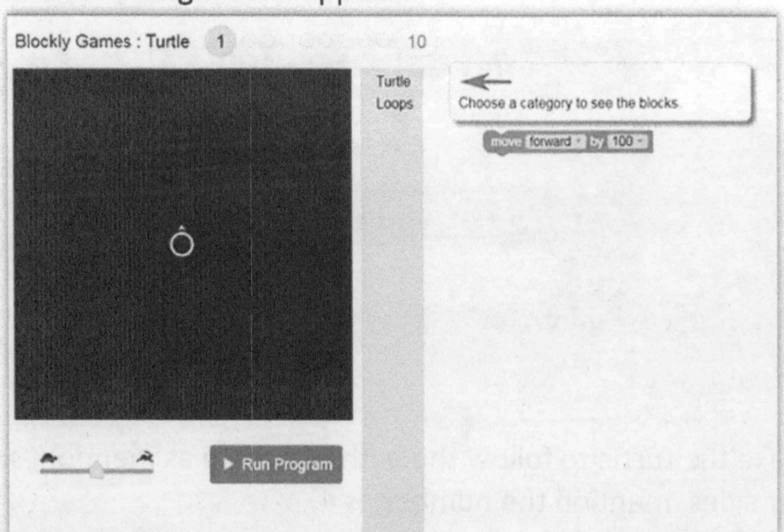

5. Click on Loops.

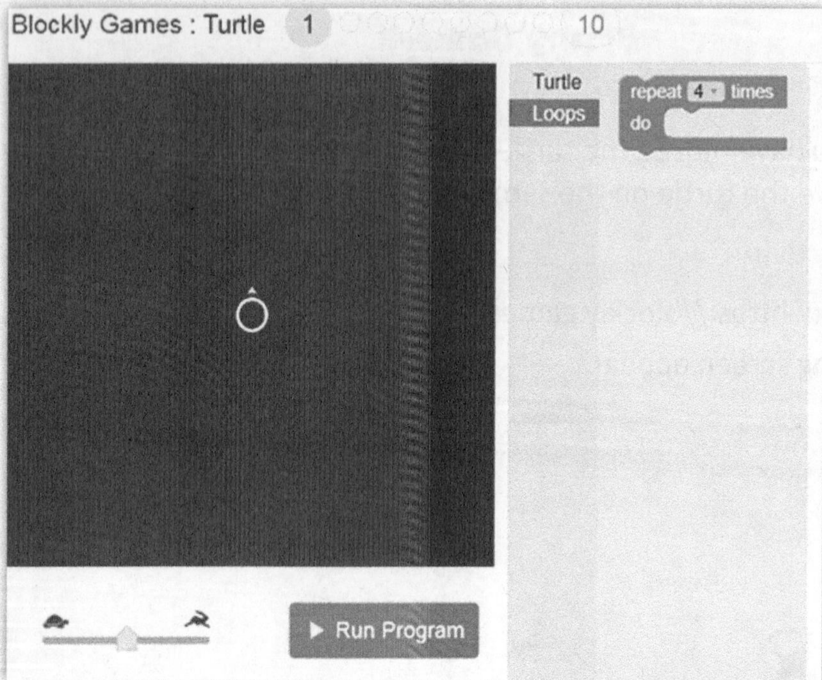

6. Drag the repeat block.

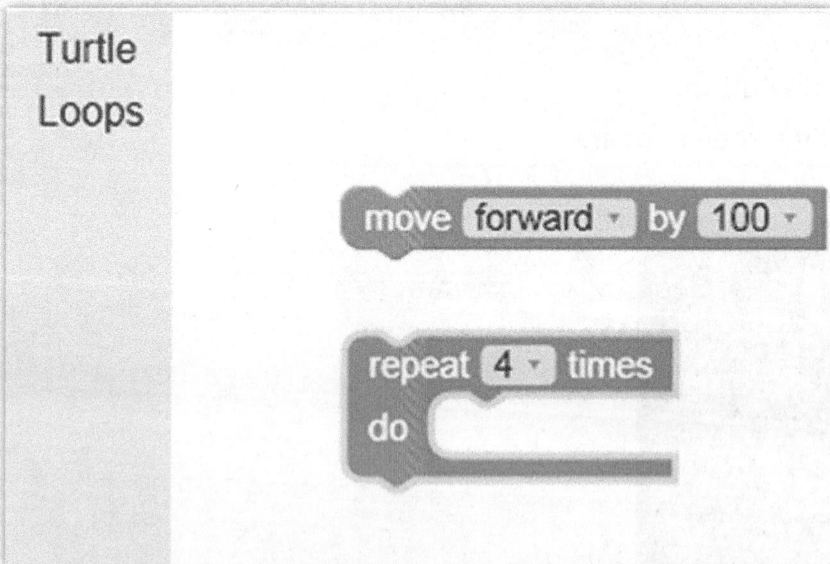

7. You have to make the turtle to follow the path of square as mention, since square has four sides, mention the number as 4.

8. Drag the move and turn block in the repeat block.

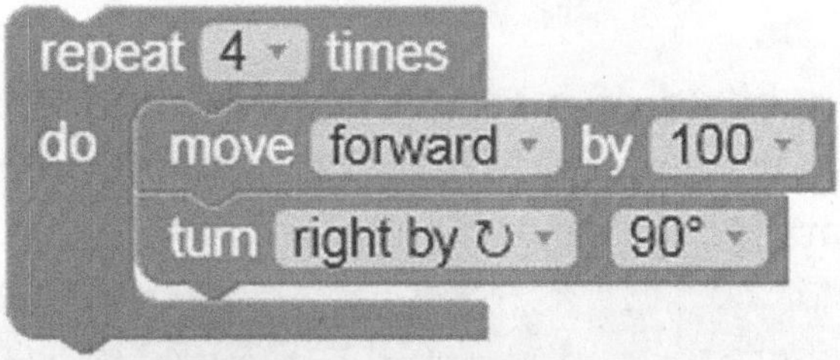

9. Click on Run Program 

.

10. You can see the turtle moves as per the instruction.

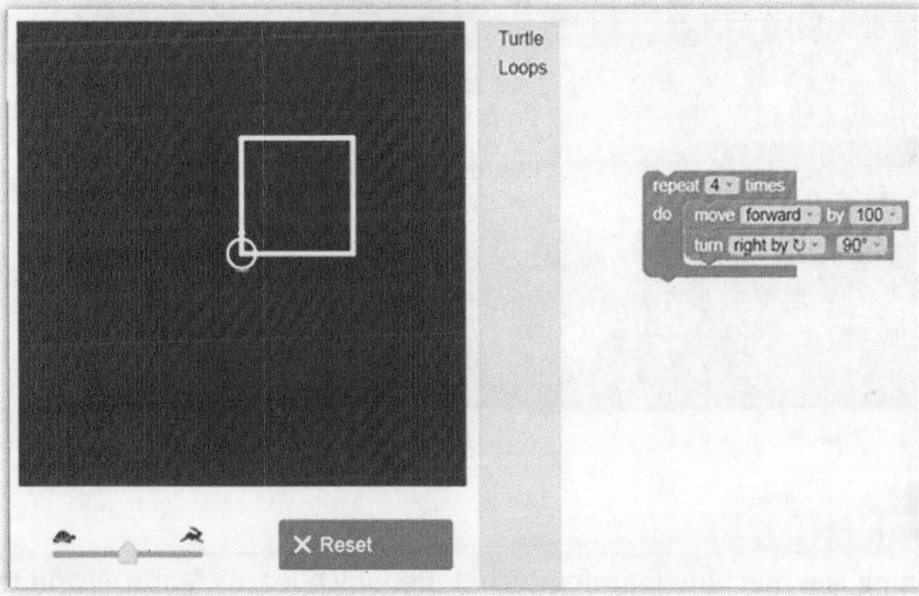

Check your Progress - II

Fill in the Blanks.

Hint: Data, Machine Learning, Artificial Intelligence

a. ________________ is a subfield of AI.

b. __________ is a subfield of computer science.

c. Machine learning enables systems to improve their performance in a given task with more and more experience or __________.

Answer: Machine Learning, Artificial Intelligence, data.

Deep Learning

Deep learning is a subfield of machine learning, and it is the complexity of a mathematical model. It's a machine learning technique which learns feature and task directly from data (image, text, file, sound).

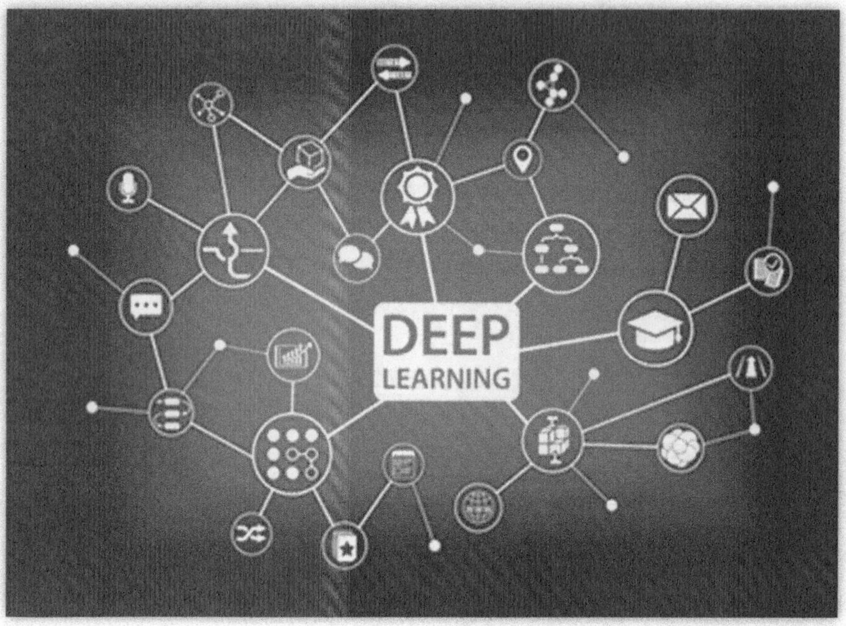

DEFINITION

Deep learning is a machine learning technique which learns features and tasks directly from data. The data can be images, text files or sound.

Applications of Deep Learning

- Object Detection or classification in photographs
- Automatic driving cars
- Automatic Game Playing
- Automatic Machine Translation
- Colorization of Black & White Images

Advantages and Disadvantages of Deep Learning

Advantages	Disadvantages
Features are automatically deduced and optimally tuned for desired outcome.	Requires very large amount of data to perform the task.
Robustness to natural variations in the data is automatically learned.	Expensive to train.
Architecture is flexible, can be adapted to new problems in the future.	Games are only poorly masked quizzes.
Neural network based approach can be applied to many different applications and data types.	Not easy to get the output as it requires classifiers.
Delivers better performance results.	Difficult to be adopted by less skilled people.

Fact Bot

Deep Learning works similarly to the human brain — Artificial Neural Networks (ANN's).

IBM Watson

Activity V

IBM Watson

Description

Watson was created as a question answering (QA) computing system by IBM to apply advanced Natural Language Processing, Information Retrieval, Knowledge Representation, Automated Reasoning, and Machine Learning technologies to the field of open domain question answering.

How it works:

It takes a question which is expressed in natural language (english), seeks to understand it in much greater detail, and returns a precise answer to the question.

When created, IBM stated that, *"more than 100 different techniques are used to analyze natural language, identify sources, find and generate hypotheses, find and score evidence, and merge and rank hypotheses."*

To perform an activity:

1. Go to the link: https://www.youtube.com/watch?v=r7E1TJ1HtM0
2. Play the video, listen how IBM Watson works and write your observation:

____

____

____

____

____

____

____

____

____

Robotics

Robotics means building and programming robots so that they can operate in complex and real-world scenarios.

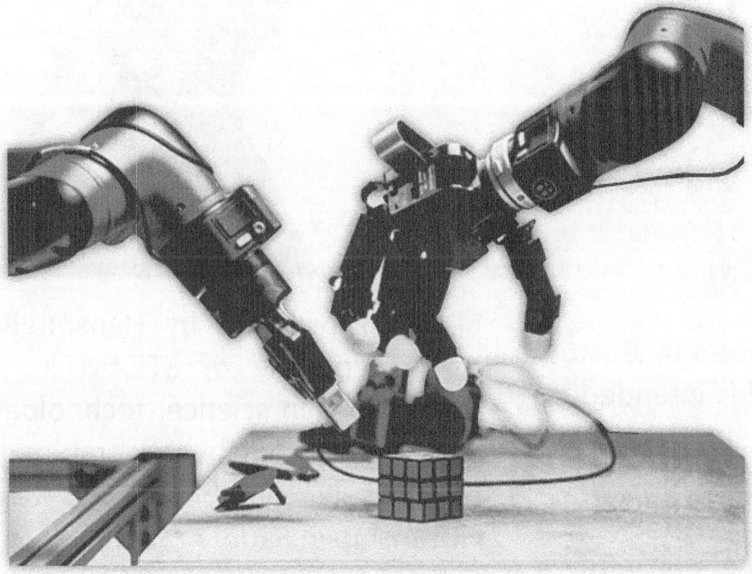

Robot

A robot is a machine which is programmed by a computer. It is capable of carrying out a complex series of actions automatically.

6 Cool Robots That Actually Exist Today

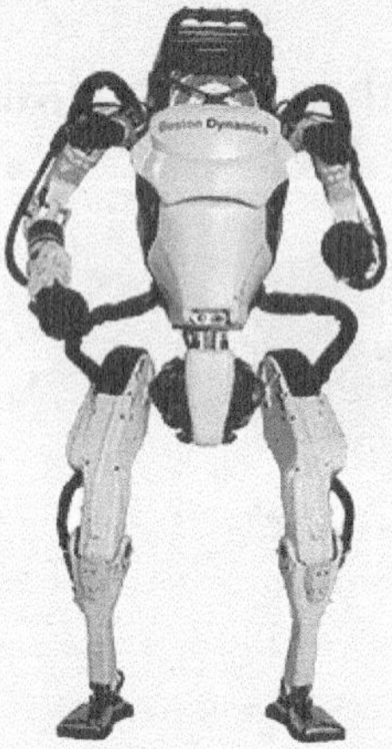

ATLAS: Developed by Boston Dynamics, and is intended to aid emergency services during search or rescue operations.

SOFIA: Developed by Hanson Robotics. Sofia is the epitome of STEAM in action, where innovations in science, technology, engineering and maths have been combined with artistry to precisely resemble us. She was even granted citizenship in Saudi Arabia!

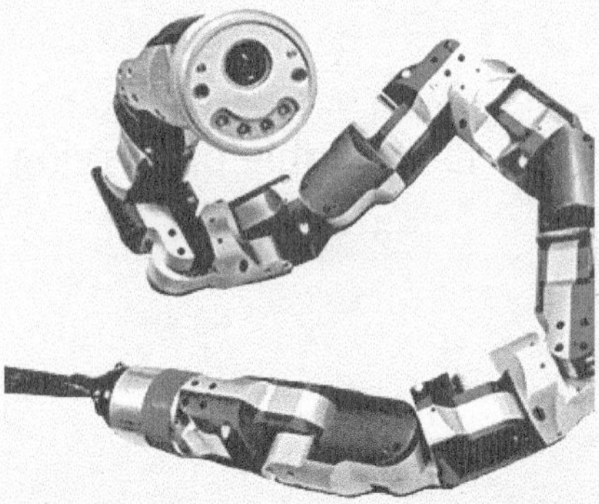

SNAKEBOT: Developed by Carnegie Mellon University and is one of the most versatile, and effective robots invented today. Resembling a snake, it is not only able to move but also climb and swim in different environments.

ASIMO (Advanced Step in Innovative Mobility): Developed by the Japanese company Honda, and has the ability to recognise moving objects, postures, gestures in the surrounding environment, as well as sounds and faces that enable interaction with humans.

MOLEY - Robot Kitchen: Developed by Moley Robotics, it can prepares and cooks food. The best thing is that it even clean up afterwards.

Aibo the Robotic Dog: Developed by Sony, it's a robotic dog that replaces real-life domestic pets. It is able to replicate many actions that provide owners with realistic experiences of owning a dog.

Tip Bot

Robots in science-fiction books, television shows, and movies can often think, listen, talk, and walk easily on two legs.

Check your Progress - III

Tick the correct option.

a. Robotics means building and programming robots so that they can operate in **simple/complex** and real-world scenarios.

b. A robot is a machine which is programmed by a **computer/animal.**

c. ATLAS robot was developed by Boston Dynamics, and is intended to aid **emergency/Day to day** services.

Answer: complex, computer, emergency

MEMORY BOT

A robot is a machine that does tasks without the help of a person.

Robot Laws

The writer Isaac Asimov told many stories about robots, who had the three mention laws of robotics to keep humans safe from them.

1. A robot may not injure a human being or, through inaction, allow a human being to come to harm.
2. A robot must obey orders given to it by human beings, except where such orders would conflict with the First Law.
3. A robot must protect its own existence as long as such protection does not conflict with the First or Second Law.

Note: These were not used in real life when Isaac Asimov invented them. However, in today's world robots are more complicated, and one day real laws may be needed, much like Isaac Asimov's original three laws.

Activity VI

Make a Robot

Description

- It is a fun activity for children of all ages!
- You need to click and drag different parts from the parts bin to the construction area to create a robot.
- You can also click on robot parts on the stage to move them around, make them bigger or smaller, and even spin them around!

Note: In this you can give your robot a special name, and type a short paragraph about your robot. Once you are finished you can print it out on one piece of paper!!!

To perform an activity:

1. Visit the link: https://www.abcya.com/games/make_a_robot

2. The following screen appears:

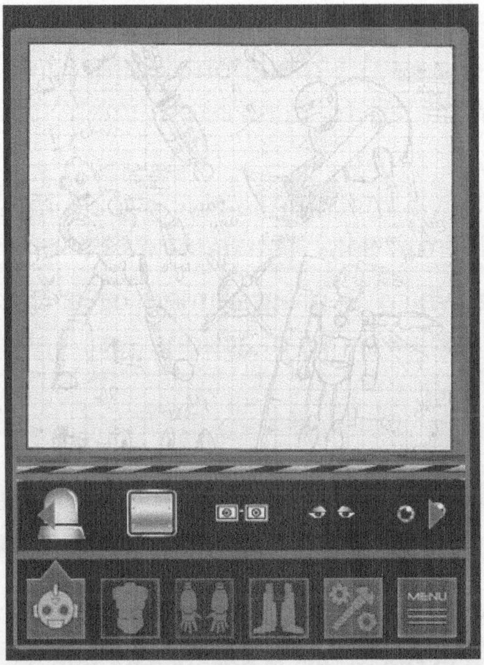

3. Build your robot by drag and drop its body parts from the option available.

Output:

4. You can save and can take print of your robot by using the available options.

Tech Bot

- **Artificial intelligence (AI):** Simulation of human intelligence in the machines which are programmed to think like humans and mimic the actions of humans.
- **Deep learning:** It is a machine learning technique which learns features and tasks directly from data. The data can be images, text files or sound.
- **Robot:** Machine which is programmed by a computer. It is capable of carrying out a complex series of actions automatically.

RECAP

- Artificial intelligence (AI) is an intelligence which is demonstrated by machines.
- The popularity of AI in the media is because people have started using the term AI when they refer to things which are called by other names.
- Science fiction stories often feature friendly humanoid servants are the things that AI provide us.
- AI field was founded on the assumption that human intelligence "can be so precisely described that a machine can be made to simulate it".
- Artificial Intelligence (AI) was first coined in 1956 at Dartmouth Conference by a cognitive scientist, John McCarthy, at the Dartmouth Conference.
- **Applications of AI**
  - Marketing
  - Agriculture
  - Health Care
  - Space Exploration
  - Chatbots
  - Social Media

- Machine Learning is a subfield of AI, and AI itself is a subfield of computer science. Machine learning enables systems to improve their performance in a given task with more and more experience or data.
- **Applications of Machine Learning**
  - Speech Recognition
  - Traffic prediction
  - Product recommendations
  - Email Spam and Malware Filtering
  - Virtual Personal Assistant
- Deep learning is a subfield of machine learning, and it is the complexity of a mathematical model.
- **Applications of Deep Learning**
  - Object Detection or classification in photographs
  - Automatic driving cars
  - Automatic Game Playing
  - Automatic Machine Translation
  - Colorization of Black & White Images
- Robotics means building and programming robots so that they can operate in complex and real-world scenarios.
- A robot is a machine which is programmed by a computer. It is capable of carrying out a complex series of actions automatically.

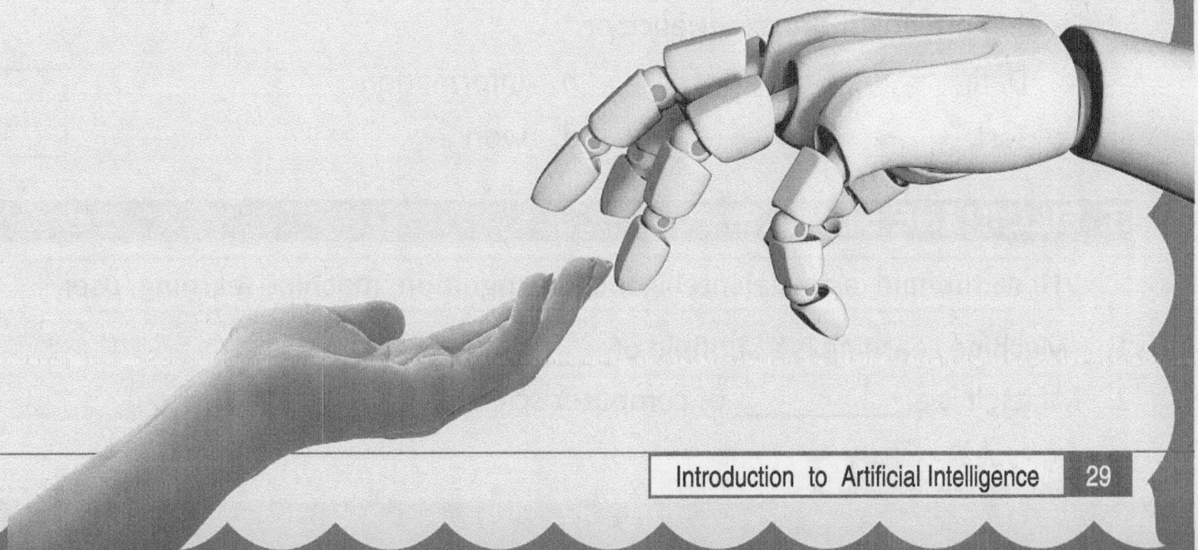

Brain Bot

A. MULTIPLE CHOICE QUESTIONS.

1. Artificial intelligence (AI) is an intelligence which is demonstrated by:
   a. Machines ☐ b. Human ☐
   c. Animal ☐ d. Objects ☐
2. You see the use of AI in:
   a. Self-driving cars ☐
   b. Content recommendation ☐
   c. Image and video processing ☐
   d. All of the above ☐
3. Artificial Intelligence (AI) was first coined in __________ at Dartmouth Conference by a cognitive scientist, John McCarthy, at the Dartmouth Conference.
   a. 1954 ☐ b. 1955 ☐
   c. 1956 ☐ d. 1957 ☐
4. Artificial intelligence (AI) refers to the simulation of human intelligence in the machines which are programmed to think like humans and mimic the actions of:
   a. Machines ☐ b. Human ☐
   c. Animal ☐ d. Objects ☐
5. Machine learning is the systems that improve the performance in a given task with more and more experience or:
   a. Data ☐ b. Information ☐
   c. Task ☐ d. work ☐

B. FILL IN THE BLANKS.

Hint: subfield, artificial Intelligence, recognition, machine learning, user

1. Machine Learning is a subfield of_____________.
2. AI itself is a ___________ of computer science.

3. __________ enables systems to improve their performance in a given task with more and more experience or data.
4. While using Google, you get an option of "Search by voice," it comes under speech_____________.
5. Product recommendations understand the ________ interest and suggests the product as per customer interest.

C. MATCH THE FOLLOWING.

Column A	Column B
1. Virtual Personal Assistant	i. Machine which is programmed by a computer
2. Deep Learning	ii. aid emergency services
3. Robot	iii. mathematical model
4. ATLAS	iv. granted citizenship in Saudi Arabia
5. SOFIA	v. Machine Learning

D. ANSWER THE FOLLOWING QUESTIONS.

1. Define the term Artificial Intelligence.

____

____

____

2. Name any two applications of Artificial Intelligence.

____

____

____

3. What is Machine learning?

____

____

____

4. What do you mean by Robotics?

____

____

____

5. Define the term Deep Learning.

____

____

____

Lab Activity Eliza, the Rogerian Therapist

Description

ELIZA is a computer program which emulates a Rogerian psychotherapist.

How it works:

You simply need to type your questions and concerns and hit return. Eliza will answer you.

To perform an activity:

1. Visit the link: http://psych.fullerton.edu/mbirnbaum/psych101/Eliza.htm
2. The following screen appears:

Eliza, the Regerian Therapist

ELIZA is a computer program that emulates a Regerian psychotherapist. Just type your questions and concerns and hit return. Eliza will answer you.

Talk to Eliza

> Hello, I am Eliza.

Input:

3. Message as "Hello, I am Eliza" appears on screen.
4. Type whatever you want to ask, Eliza will give you the answer.

Talk to Eliza

> Hello, I am Eliza.

* hi

> How are you today.. What would you like to discuss?

* I would like to discuss about Artificial Intelligence.

> Can you elaborate on that?

Input:

WORKSHEET

A. STATE WHETHER THE FOLLOWING STATEMENT ARE TRUE OR FALSE.

1. Self-driving cars works on combination of AI technique. True / False
2. AI is not used to generate or alter visual content. True / False
3. Automatic methods for search and planning were considered to belong to the domain of AI. True / False
4. Science fiction stories often feature friendly humanoid servants are the things that computer provide us. True / False
5. AI research concentrated on automated tasks, and encapsulate the essence of intelligence. True / False

B. FILL IN THE BLANKS.

Hints: AI, simulate, voice, human intelligence, John McCarthy

1. AI field was founded on the assumption that human intelligence "can be so precisely described that a machine can be made to __________ it".
2. Artificial Intelligence (AI) was first coined in 1956 at Dartmouth Conference by a cognitive scientist, __________, at the Dartmouth Conference.
3. Artificial intelligence (AI) refers to the simulation of __________ in the machines which are programmed to think like humans and mimic the actions of humans.
4. When it comes to saving our lives, a lot of organizations and medical care centres are relying on __________.
5. Virtual Personal Assistant helps you in finding the information using your __________ instruction.

C. ANSWER THE FOLLOWING QUESTIONS.

1. Define the use of Machine learning in Email filtering.

2. What is the main goal of Deep Learning?

3. Name any two applications of Robots.

4. Write any one advantage and disadvantage of Machine Learning.

5. Write any two application of Deep Learning.

Quiz Card

TICK THE CORRECT ANSWER.

1. Artificial intelligence is:
   a. Giving intelligence to Computer
   b. Program yourself
   c. Making a Machine intelligent
   d. Putting more and more memory to Computer

2. Artificial Intelligence can be used in:
   a. Planning and Scheduling　　b. Game Playing
   c. Robotics　　d. All of the above

3. Computer system capable of thinking, reasoning and learning is known is
   a. Machine intelligence　　b. Human intelligence
   c. Artificial intelligence　　d. Virtual intelligence

4. __________ was originally called the "imitation game" by its creator.
   a. The Turing Test　　b. LISP
   c. The Logic Theorist　　d. Cybernetics

5. Who is known as the -Father of AI"?
   a. Fisher Ada　　b. Alan Turing
   c. John McCarthy　　d. Allen Newell

6. The conference that launched the AI revolution in 1956 was held at?
   a. Dartmouth　　b. Harvard
   c. New York　　d. Stanford

7. A robot's "arm" is also known as its __________
   a. end effector　　b. actuator
   c. manipulator　　d. servomechanism

8. What will take place as the agent observes its interactions with the world?
   a. Learning　　b. Hearing
   c. Perceiving　　d. Speech

9. Which modifies the performance element so that it makes better decision?
   a. Performance element　　b. Changing element
   c. Learning element　　d. None of the above

10 How many things are concerned in the design of a learning element?
   a. 1　　b. 2
   c. 3　　d. 4

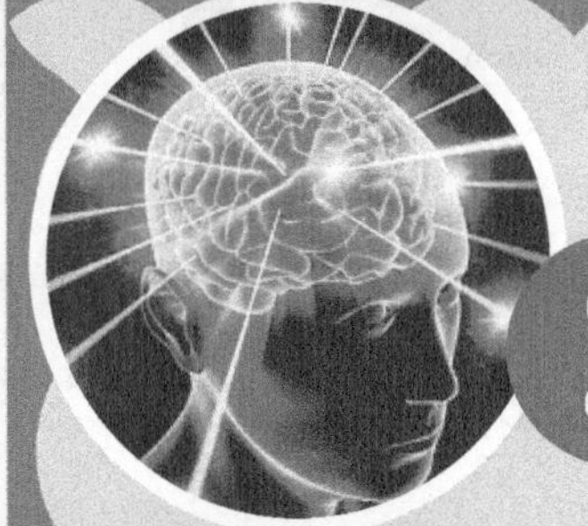

2 ARTIFICIAL INTELLIGENCE PROBLEM SOLVING IN REAL WORLD

Structure Bot

In this chapter, we will discuss:

- Search and problem solving
- Solving problems with AI
- Search and games

Objective Bot

At the end of this chapter, you should be able to:

- Know the Odds and Probability
- Learn about the Bayes rule
- Understand the meaning of Game Tree

Introduction to Search and Problem Solving

Consider an example, suppose you want to go from point A to B, by using Public transport.

What do you do? You will pull out your Smartphone, type the destination and start following the instructions.

This situation is using Search and Planning Problems.

Toy Problem: Chicken Crossing

Consider a situation; In this a robot is on a rowboat who needs to move a fox, a chicken, and a sack of chicken-feed across a river. The problem is this, if robot moves fox – chicken & chicken – chicken feed together, the fox will eat the chicken if it has the chance, and the chicken will eat the chicken-feed if it has the chance, and both is not a desirable outcome.

So, the robot need to take care of the animals from doing harm when it is near them, but only the robot can operate the rowboat and only two of the pieces of cargo can fit on the rowboat together with the robot.

Think...How can the robot move all of its cargo to the opposite bank of the river?

Solution:

The Robot and the chicken cross the river, (the fox and Chicken feed are safe together), now the robot will leave the chicken on the other side and goes back across.

Robot then takes the fox across the river, and since robot can't leave the fox and chicken together, he brings the chicken back.

Again, since the chicken and chicken feed can't be left together, robot leaves the chicken and he takes the chicken feed across and leaves it with the fox.

Robot then returns to pick up the chicken and heads across the river one last time.

State Space, Transitions, and Costs

To formalize a planning problem, we must use the concepts of state space, transitions, and costs.

- **The state space:** The set of possible situations.
- **Transitions:** Possible moves between one state to another.
- **Costs:** Time/Money required to complete the task

Fact Bot

Artificial intelligence (AI) is making a computer thinks like a human to be able to learn and to have new ideas.

Activity I

Tower of Hanoi

Description

The Tower of Hanoi is a mathematical game or puzzle. It consists of three rods and disks of different sizes, which can slide onto any rod. Initially the disk are arrange in ascending order of size on one rod, the smallest at the top, thus making a conical shape.

The objective of the puzzle is to move the entire stack to last rod, and rules to play solve the puzzle is:

- Only one disk can be moved at a time.
- Each move consists of taking the upper disk from one of the stacks and placing it on top of another stack or on an empty rod.

- No larger disk may be placed on top of a smaller disk.
- With 3 disks, the puzzle can be solved in 7 moves.

To perform an activity:

1. Go to the link: https://www.mathsisfun.com/games/towerofhanoi.html
2. The following screen appears:

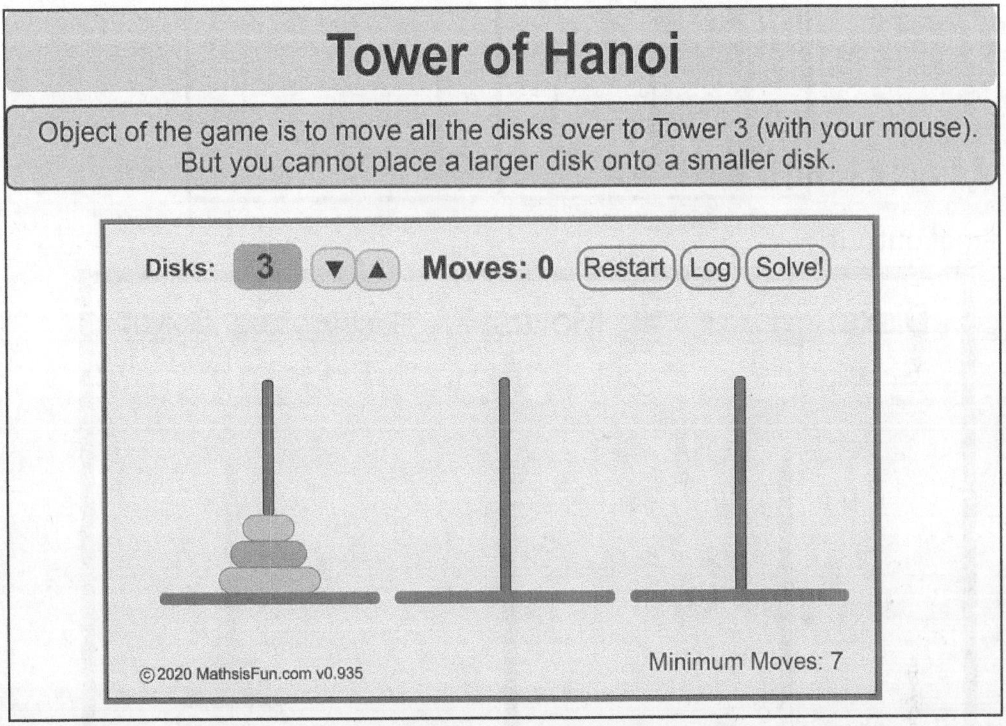

3. Now, you have to move the three disk to tower three, keeping in mind that larger disk cannot be placed on the smaller disk.

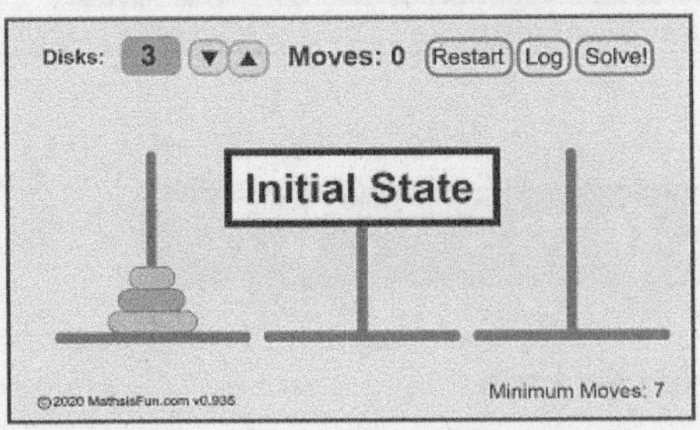

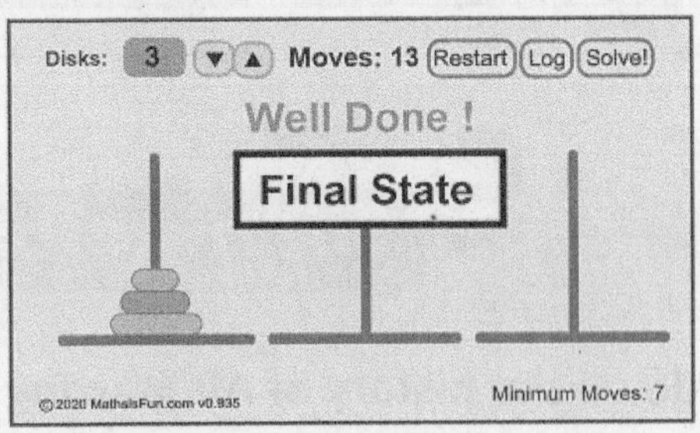

4. Start moving the disk, as shown:

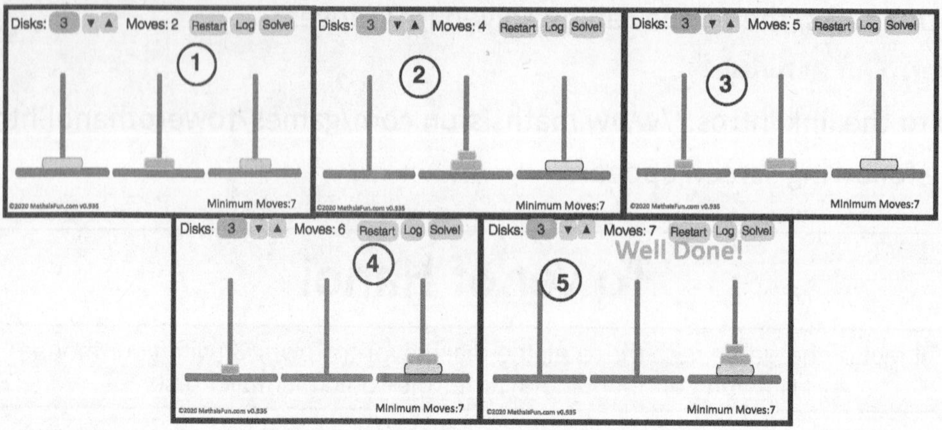

5. Final output:

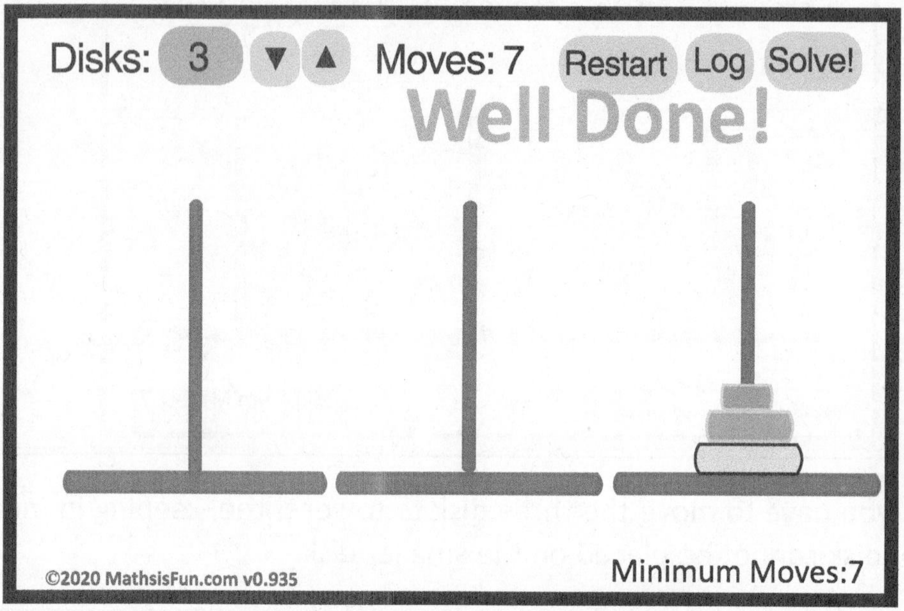

Solving Problems with AI

Interlude on the history of AI: Starting from Search

AI is as old as computer science. Long before we had computers, people thought of the possibility of Automatic Reasoning and Intelligence.

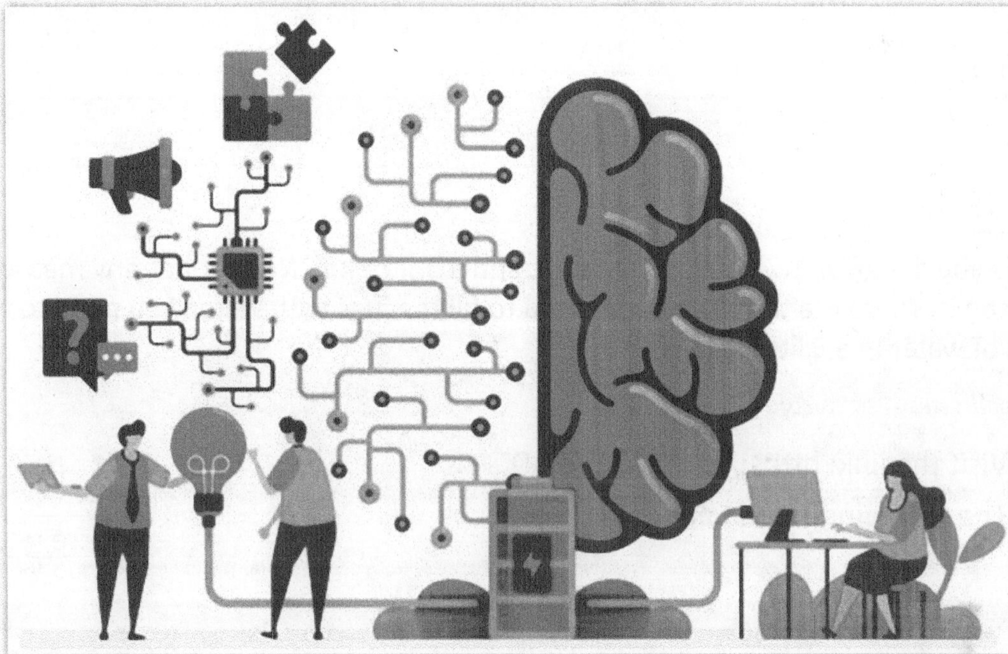

Alan Turing designed a very simple device which can compute anything which is computable and the device is known as the **Turing machine**. Machine lead Turing to the invention of programmable computers that can be used to carry out different tasks depending on what they were programmed to do.

So, instead of having to build a different device for each task, we use the same computer for many tasks. This is the idea of programming.

According to **John McCarthy** any element of intelligence can be broken down into small steps so that each of the steps is simple and "mechanical" that it can be written down as a computer program.

Search and planning techniques were an area where AI lead to great advances in the 1960s: algorithms were developed then, and are still the basis for game playing.

DEFINITION

Turing test: AI does not mean to make a computer smart just by knowing more information. AI is to build a machine that can act as if it were smart and seem more human.

Activity II

Water Jug Problem

Description

In this you are given two jugs, a 5 litre jug and a 3-litre jug. Neither has any measuring mark on it. There is a tap that can be used to fill the jugs with water. You need to get 4 litres of water in a 5 litre jug.

To perform an activity:

1. Visit the link: https://bit.ly/31CqTjD
2. The following screen appears:

Litre = 'L'

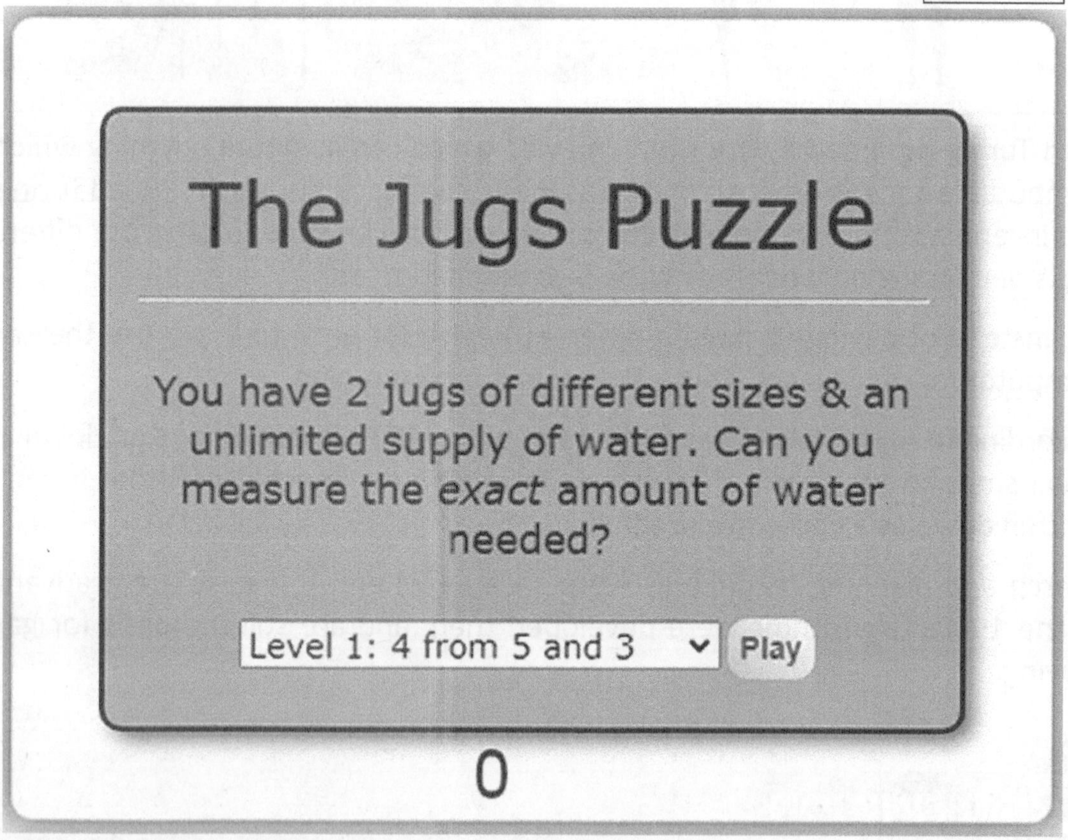

3. Click on Play and the following screen appears:

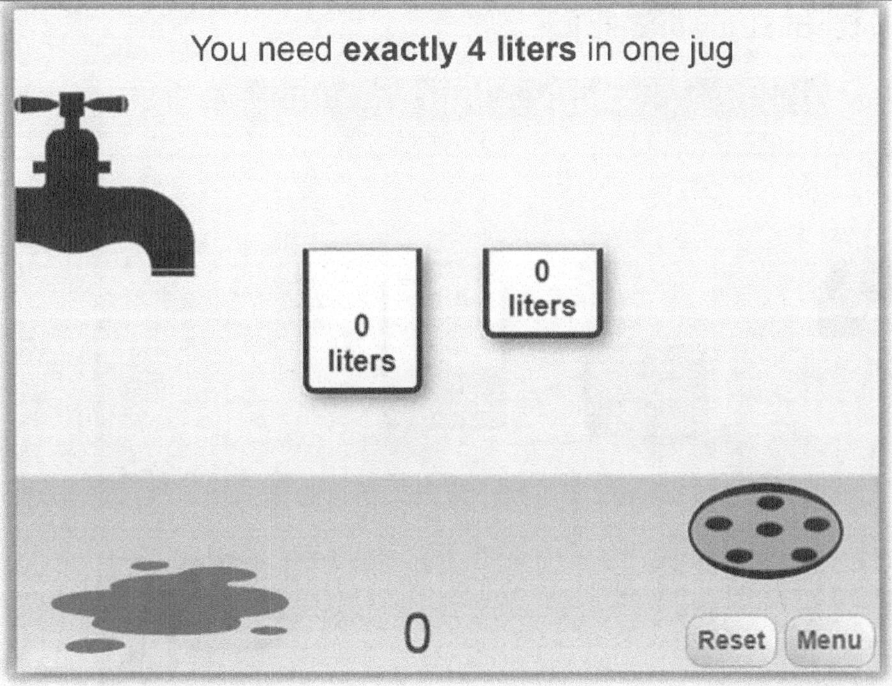

4. Now you have to fill 4L of water to big jug which is of 5L, with the help of small jug which is of 3L.
5. Fill big jug.

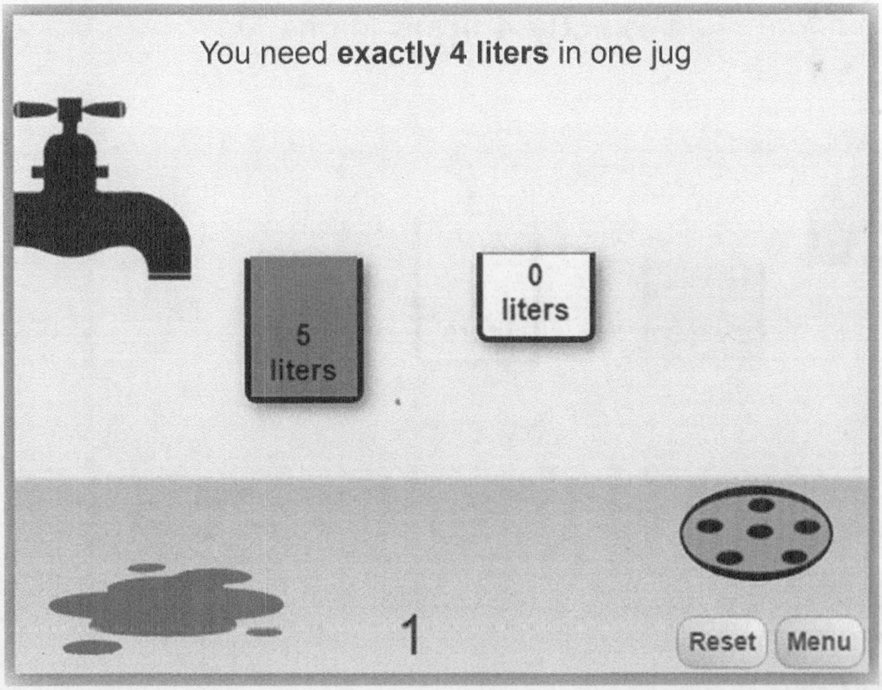

6. Put the water of 5L jug into 3L jug.

7. Empty the 5L jug.

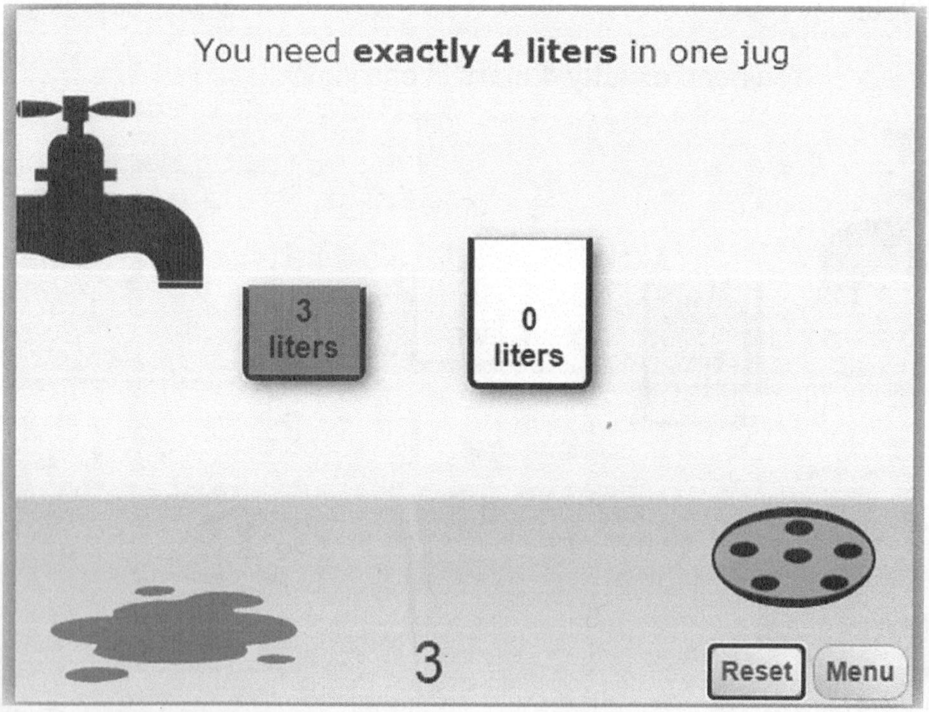

8. Put 3L of water into 5L jug.

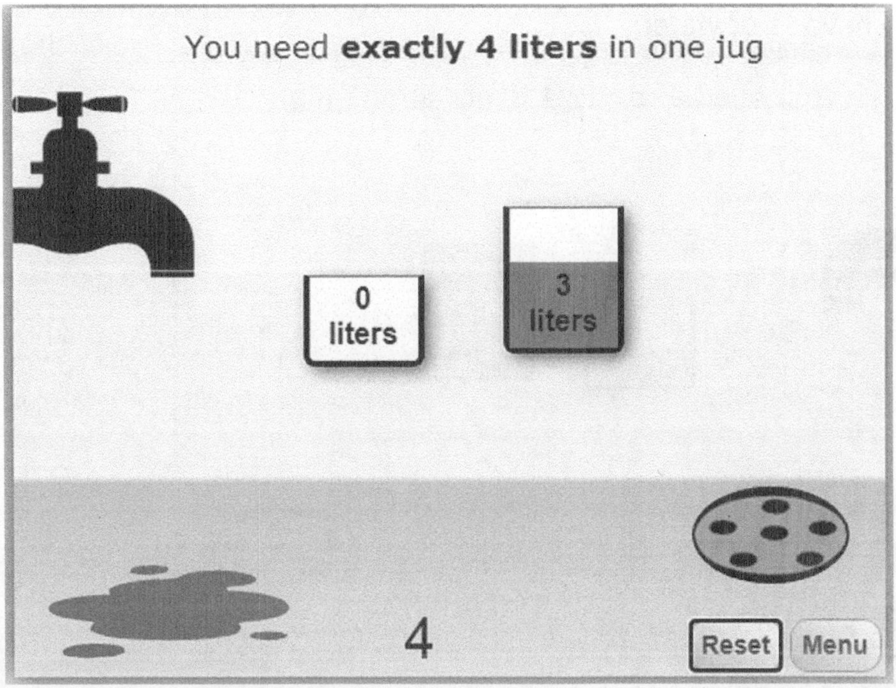

9. Fill small jug with water.

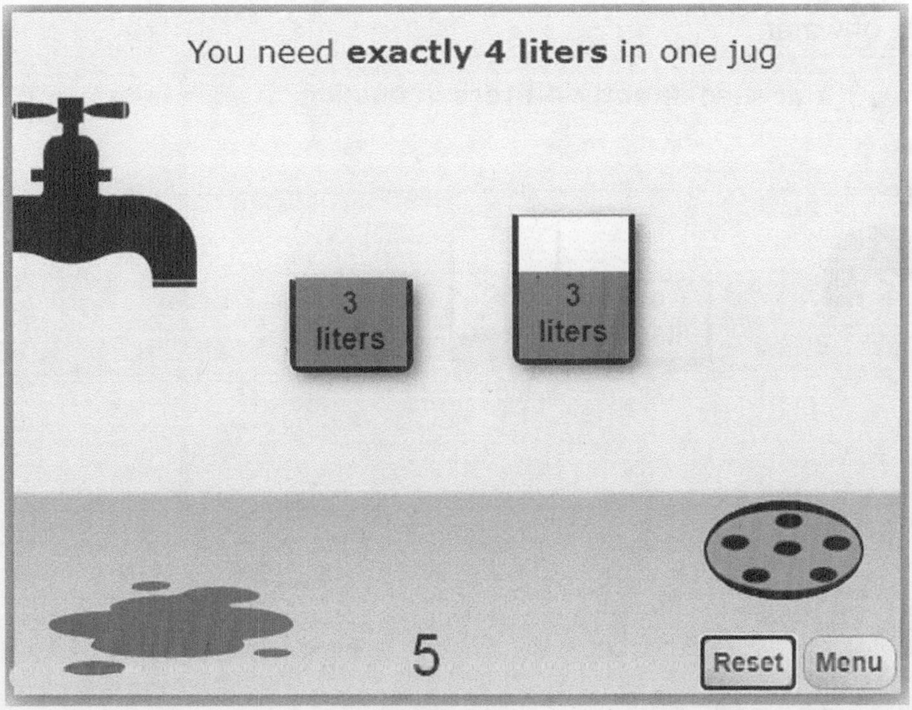

10. Pour the water of small jug of 3L into big jug. And you can see that small jug will now have 1L of water.

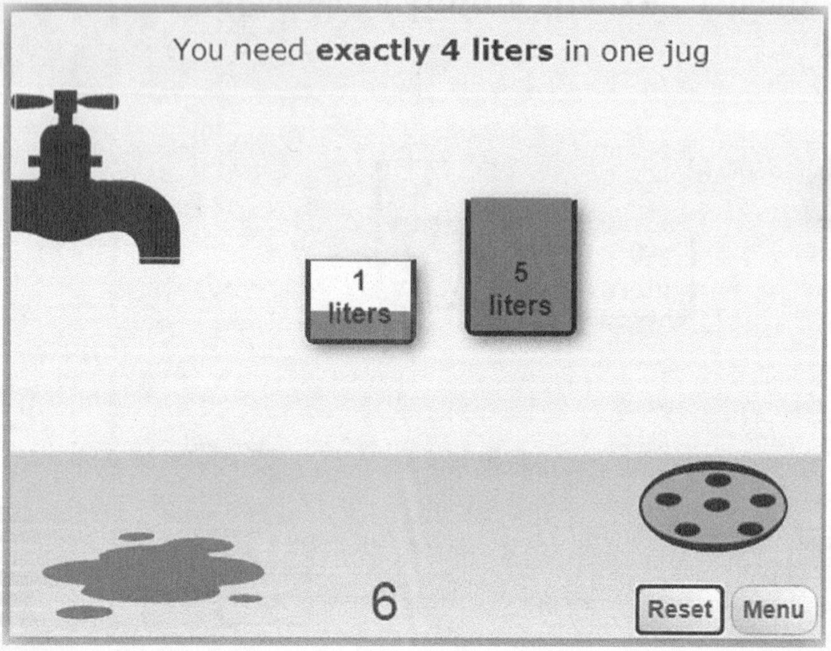

11. Empty 5L jug, and transfer the water of small jug to big jug. Now the big jug have 1L of water.

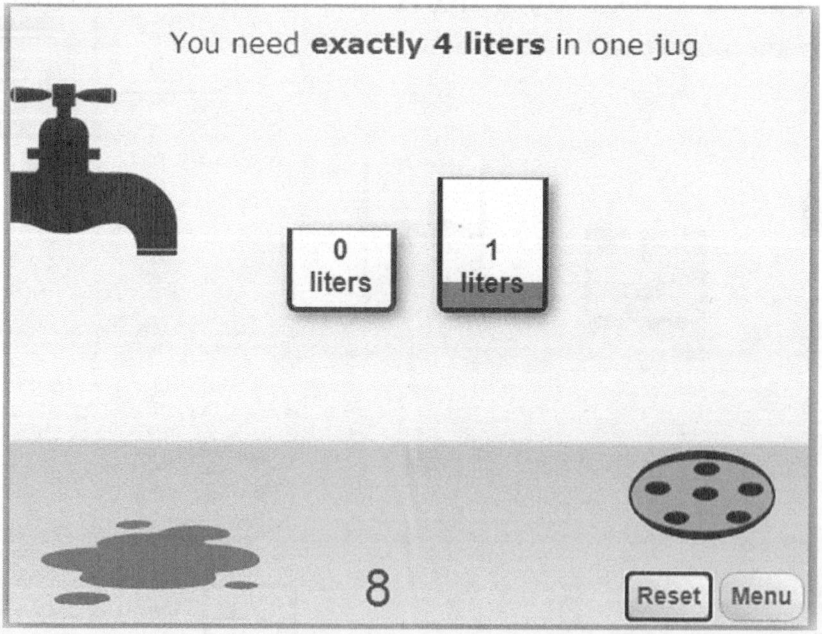

12. Fill the small jug with water and transfer the 3L of water to big jug.

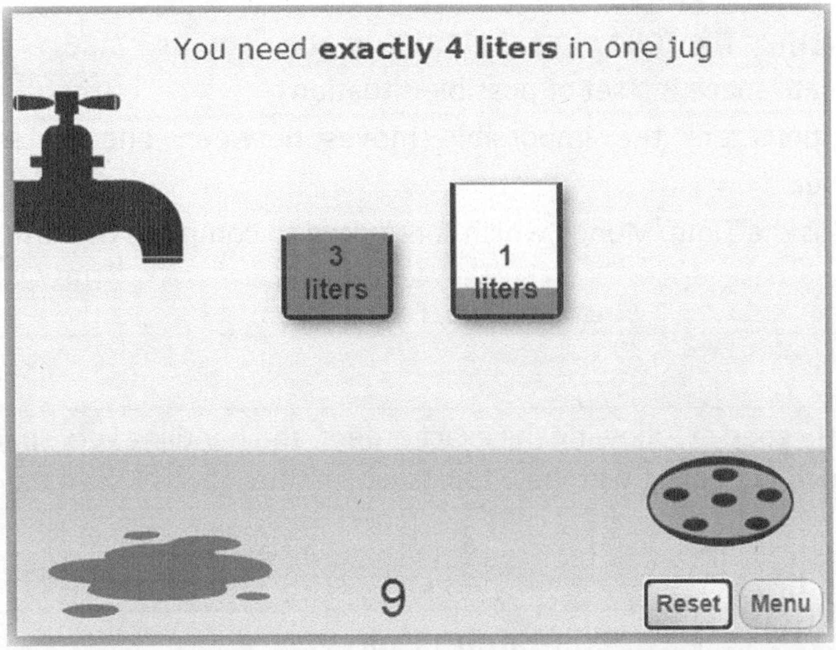

13. You can see the big jug which is of 5L, now have 4L of water.

Check your Progress - I

State whether the following statements are True or False.

a. The state space is a set of possible situations. True / False

b. Transitions are the impossible moves between one states to another. True / False

c. Costs is the Time/Money which is required to complete the task. True / False

Answer: True, False, True

Tip Bot

Computers are very good at following the exact orders, and handling very specific things, but not good at dealing with new things which they haven't seen before.

Activity III

Pattern Match - Colors

Description

In this you need to identify the pattern and draw the similar pattern to cross the level.

To perform an activity:

1. Visit the link: https://bit.ly/3sBg1i5
2. The following screen appears:

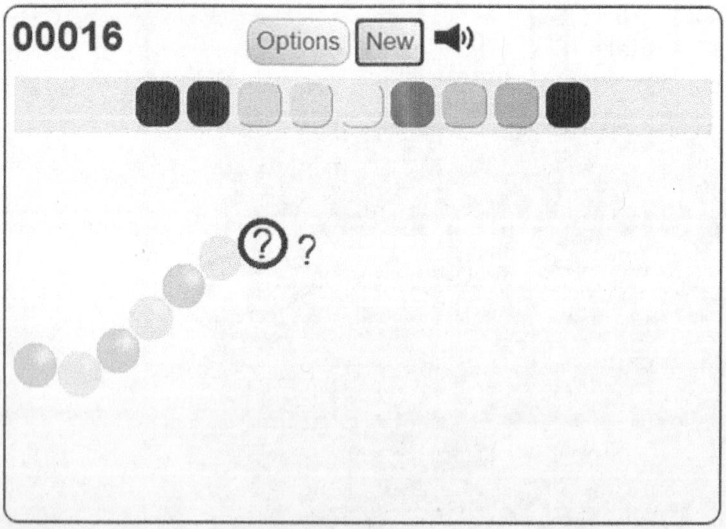

3. Identify and draw the pattern of Blue and Yellow balls.

4.

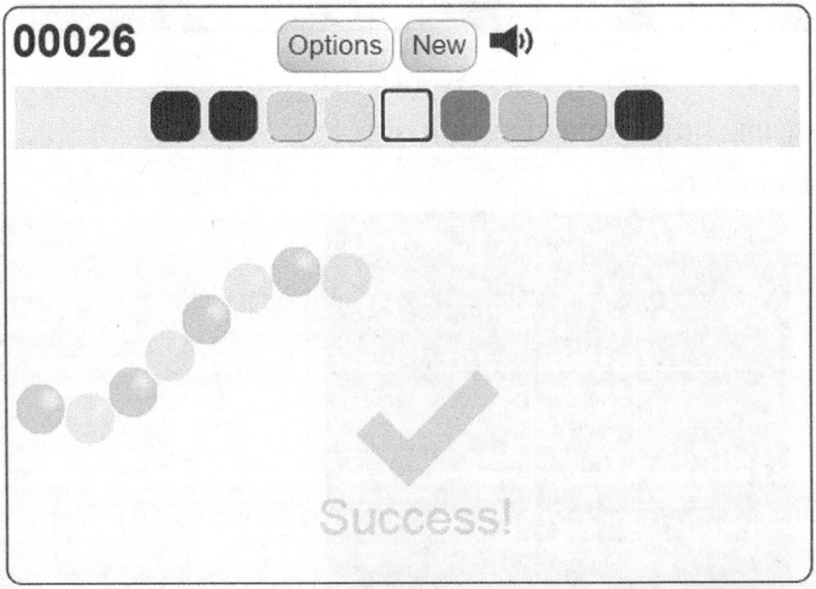

MEMORY BOT

AI is meant to be a simulation of human intelligence.

Search and Games

Consider an example of Playing Tic Tac Toe game.

Activity IV

Tic-tac-toe game

Tic-tac-toe: Noughts and Crosses or Xs and Os, is a paper-and-pencil game for two players, X and O. In this player play turn by turn, and mark the spaces in a 3×3 grid. The player who succeeds in placing three of their marks in a diagonal, horizontal, or vertical row is the winner. It is a solved game with a forced draw assuming best play from both players.

GamePlay: To win the game, a player must place three of their marks in a horizontal, vertical, or diagonal row.

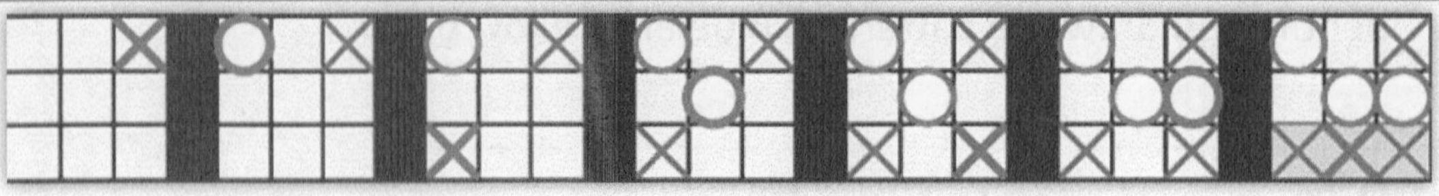

To perform an activity:

1. Go to the following link: https://playtictactoe.org/
2. The following page appears:

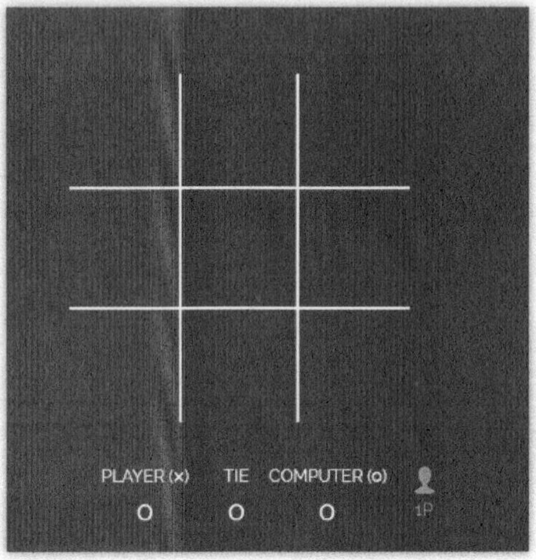

3. Start playing the game and try to mark the three X's in horizontal, vertical or diagonal row, similarly your opponent (computer in this case) also try to mark its 0's to win the game.

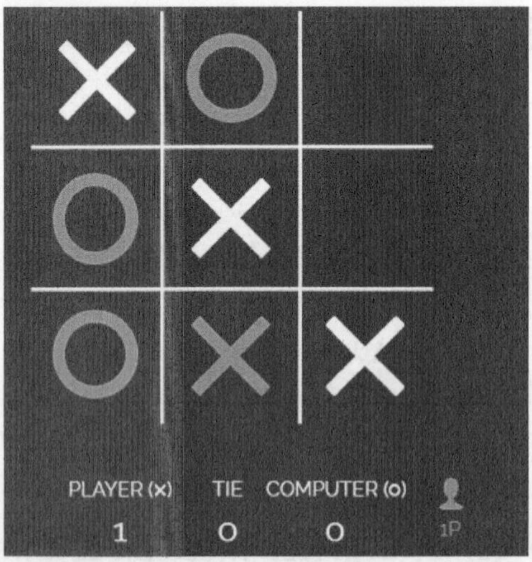

4. In case, if nobody makes horizontal, vertical or diagonal row, the game get Tie.

Game trees

To solve games using AI, the concept of a game tree is introduced. The different states of the game are represented by nodes in the game tree, which is very similar to the planning problems. In the game tree, the nodes are arranged in levels that correspond to each player's turns in the game so that the "root" node of the tree is the beginning position in the game.

In tic-tac-toe game as shown in Activity IV, this would be the empty grid with no Xs or Os played yet. Under root, on the second level, there are the possible states that can result from the first player's moves, be it X or O. We call these nodes the "children" of the root node.

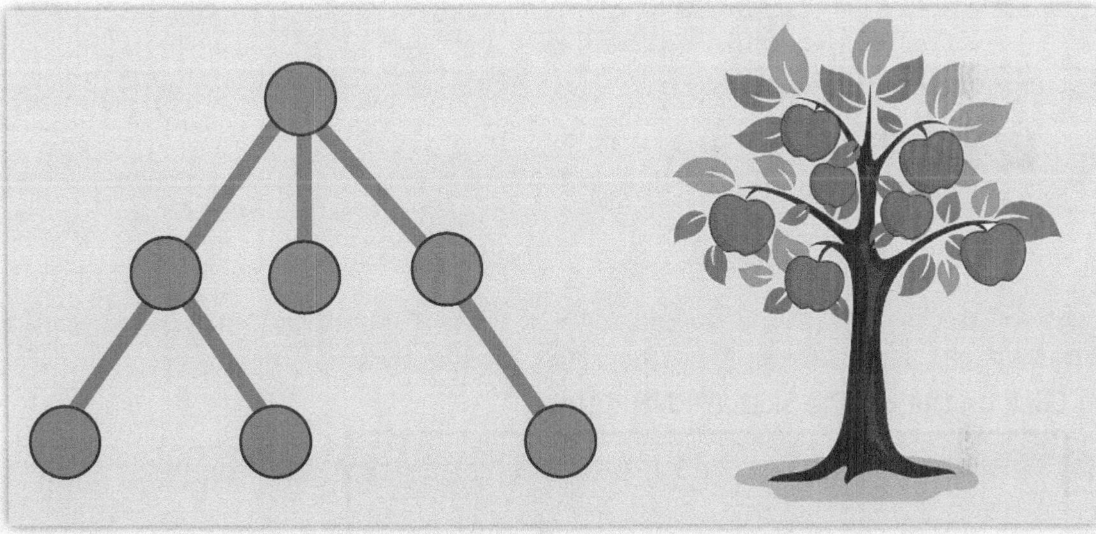

Each node on the second level, would further have as its children nodes the states that can be reached from it by the opposing player's moves. This is continued, level by level, until reaching states where the game is over. In tic-tac-toe, this means that either one of the players gets a line of three and wins, or the board is full and the game ends in a tie.

DEFINITION

Game tree: Directed graph whose nodes are positions in a game and whose edges are the moves.

Activity V

Sketch-RNN (Draw Single Image)

In this, you will draw an image with a recurrent neural network model. Once you start drawing the object, Sketch-RNN will provide many possible ways to continue drawing form where you left off.

To perform an activity:

1. Go to the link: https://experiments.withgoogle.com/sketch-rnn-demo
2. Click on Launch Experiment.

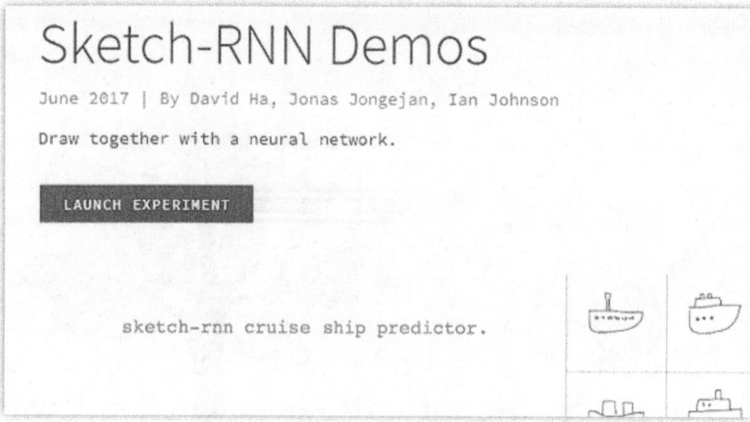

3. Click on the try the Sketch-RNN demo.

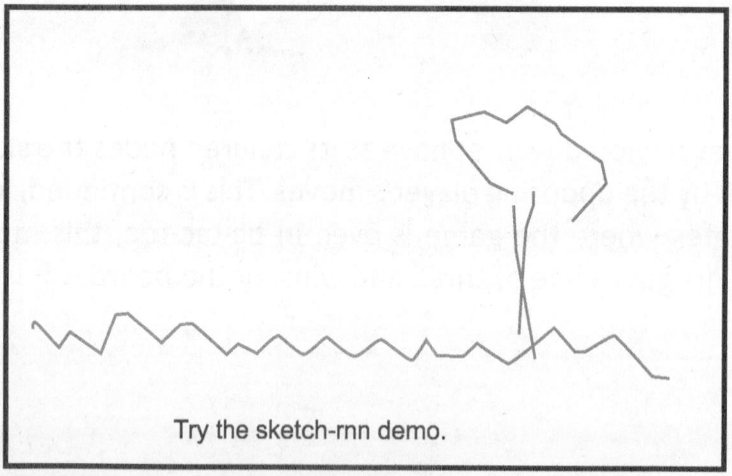

4. You can see the following screen:

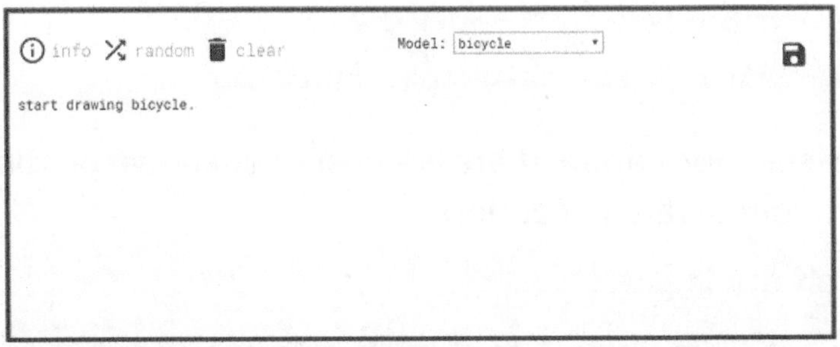

5. We have selected model as Bicycle in the box.
6. The message as Start drawing bicycle appears.
7. Start drawing the bicycle in the given space.

8. Where you stop drawing, it will automatically complete the picture:

Fact Bot

Artificial Intelligence is when a computer program or machine has the ability to think and learn.

Odds and Probability

In real world instead of perfect information, there is a host of unknown possibilities from missing information to deliberate deception.

Consider an example of Self-driving car:

In this you set the goal to get from point A to B in an efficient and safe manner which follows all laws. But what happens if the traffic gets worse than expected?

So, A self-driving car needs to use a variety of sensors, which may be sonar-like ones and cameras, to detect where it is and what is around it. These sensors are never perfect as the data from the sensors may includes some errors and inaccuracies called "noise". It is very common then that one sensor indicates that the road ahead turns left, but another sensor indicates the opposite direction. This needs to be resolved without always stopping the car in case of even a slightest amount of noise.

Tip Bot

Sophia is a realistic humanoid robot which is capable of displaying human-like expressions and interacting with people.

So, in this case the Probability and Odds are:

Odds:

- Sensors may not work properly for one second.
- Internet is not working.

Probability:

- Car going in front suddenly applies a break.
- Suddenly animal comes in front of car.
- Roads are under maintenance.
- Unexpected traffic.
- Traffic lights are not working.

MEMORY BOT

AI creates an opportunity to bridge the gap between virtual and physical sales channels.

Akinator

Akinator is a computer game and mobile app which was developed by French company Elokence. During gameplay, it attempts to determine what fictional or real-life character, object, film, television show, or animal the player is thinking of by asking a series of questions. It uses an artificial intelligence program which learns the best questions to ask through its experience with players.

Gameplay

- To begin the questionnaire, you need to press the play button and think of a popular character, object or other things that frequently come to mind.
- Akinator, a cartoon genie, begins asking a series of questions , with "Yes", "No", "Probably", "Probably not" and "Don't know" as possible answers, to identify the potential character.
- If the answer is narrowed down to a single likely option before 25 questions are asked, the program will automatically ask whether the character it choose is correct or not.
- If the character is guessed wrong three times in a row, then the program will prompt the user to input the character's name, to expand its database of choices.

To play the game:

1. Visit the link: https://en.akinator.com/
2. The following screen appears:

3. Click on PLAY, next screen will ask you to choose the game thematic.

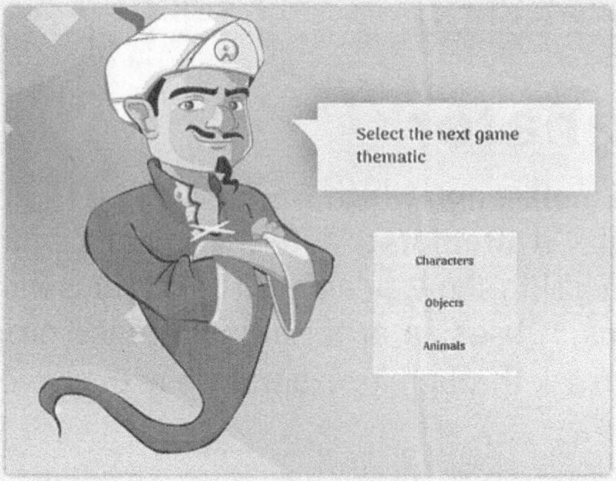

4. We have chosen: Objects.
5. Now jinni will ask you around 20-25 questions, and will guess the name of the object chosen based on your answers. You will need to answer the questions in "Yes", "No", "Probably", "Probably not" and "Don't know".

6. After you answer the questions asked by jinni, then jinni will guess the name of the object.

7. If the guess is correct then click on Yes, and if it is not, then click on No.
8. In case if you click on Yes, then the game stop here, and in case if you press No, then jinni will ask further questions to identify the object.

Check your Progress - II

Fill in the Blanks.

Hint: game tree, nodes, levels

a. To solve games using AI, the concept of _________ is introduced.

b Different states of the game are represented by ________in the game tree.

c In the game tree, the nodes are arranged in ________ that correspond to each player's turns in the game

Answer: nodes , levels, game tree

The Bayes Rule/ Bayes Formula

The Bayes rule can be expressed in many forms. One of the simplest form to express it is in terms of odds. In this we need to take the odds for something which is happening which we'll call prior odds.

DEFINITION

Bayes Theorem provides a principled way for calculating a conditional probability.

Consider an example:

The chances that it will rain later today? Imagine getting up in the morning and the chances of rain are 206 days out of 365 days. The number of days without rain is therefore 159. This converts to prior odds of 206:159 for rain, so the cards are stacked against you already before you open your eyes.

Imagine after opening your eyes and taking a look outside, you notice it's cloudy. So, imagine the chances of having a cloudy morning on a rainy day are 9 days out of 10 days – that means that only one out of 10 rainy days start out with blue skies. But sometimes there are also clouds without rain: the chances of having clouds on a rainless day are 1 in 10. Now how much higher are the chances of clouds on a rainy day compared to a rainless day?

The chances of clouds are nine times higher on a rainy day than on a rainless day: on a rainy day the chances are 9 out of 10, whereas on a rainless day the chances of clouds are 1 out of 10, and that makes nine times higher.

Note that even though the two probabilities 9/10 and 1/10 sum up to 9/10 + 1/10 = 1, this is by no means always the case. In some other town, the mornings of rainy days could be cloudy eight times out of ten. This, however, would not mean that the rainless days are cloudy two times out of ten.

Tip Bot

An ex-NASA engineer created and built a robot named Skippa that can skip a rock over 60 times!

Check your Progress - III

Tick the correct option.

a. Simplest form to express Bayes rule is in terms of **odds/even.**

b. Bayes Theorem provides a principled way for calculating a **optional/conditional** probability.

c. The Bayes rule can be expressed in **one/many** forms.

Answer: odds, conditional, many.

Fact Bot

Bayes Theorem is a principled way of calculating a conditional probability without the joint probability.

Activity VI

Semantris Game

Description

In this game, you will get words for hint, you need to type similar word, AI system will guess the connections among the word which you have typed and the words adjoin that will disappear from the list of words. Your score will be updated on the basics of the eliminated words.

Semantris is a set of word association games powered by machine-learned, natural language understanding technology. Each time you enter a clue, the AI looks at all the words in play and chooses the ones it thinks are most related. Because the AI was trained on billions of examples of conversational text that span a large variety of topics, it's able to make many types of associations.

To perform an activity:

1. Visit the link: https://experiments.withgoogle.com/semantris
2. The following screen appears:

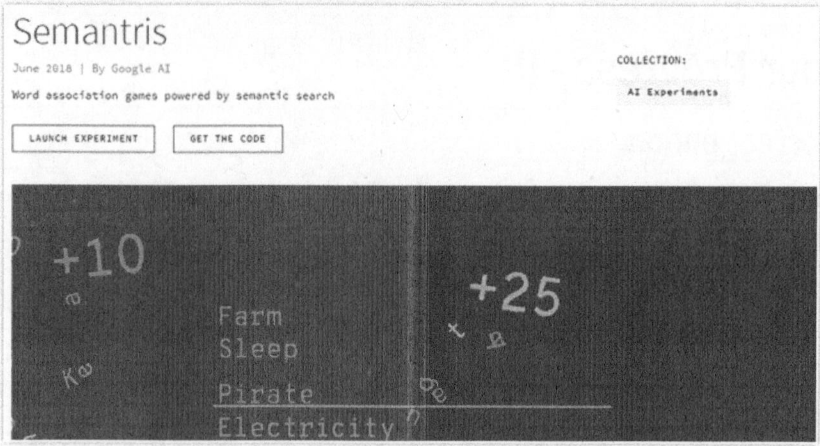

3. Click on LAUNCH EXPERIMENT, and the following screen appears:

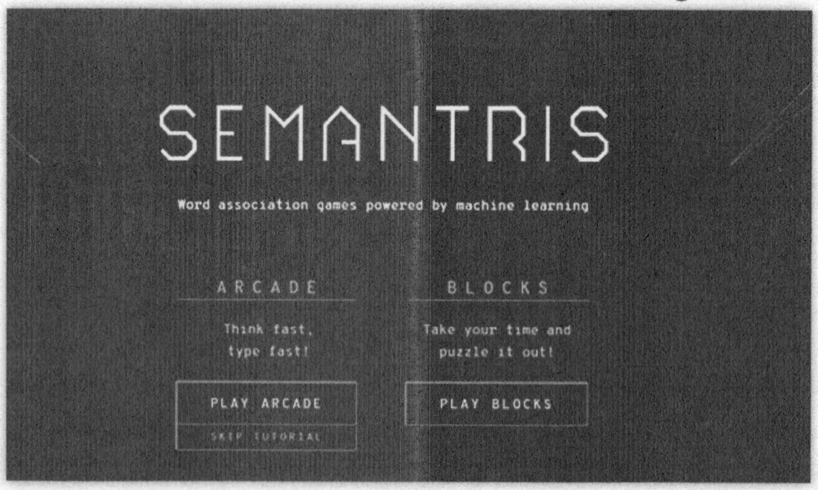

4. You can either choose ARCADE or BLOCKS. (We have chosen ARCADE).
5. The following screen appears:

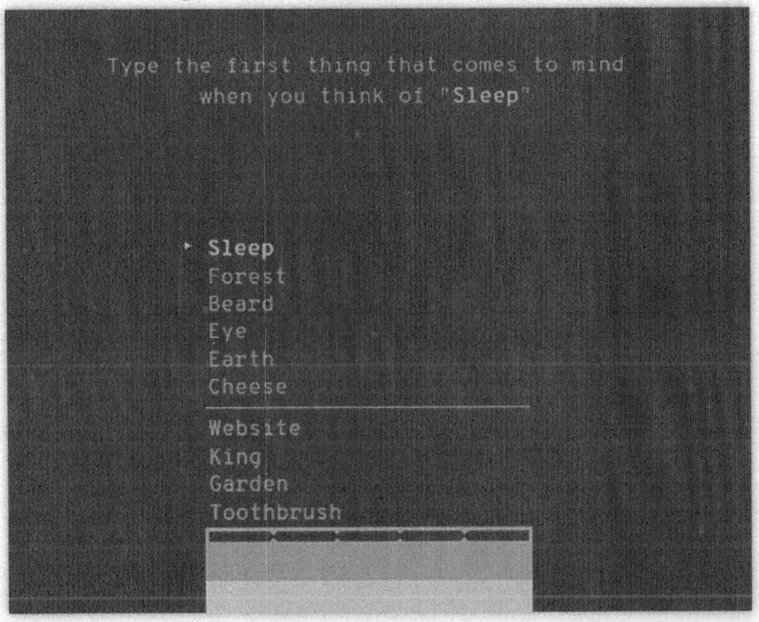

6. Arrow is on Sleep, you need to write word related to sleep.
7. We have written Night.

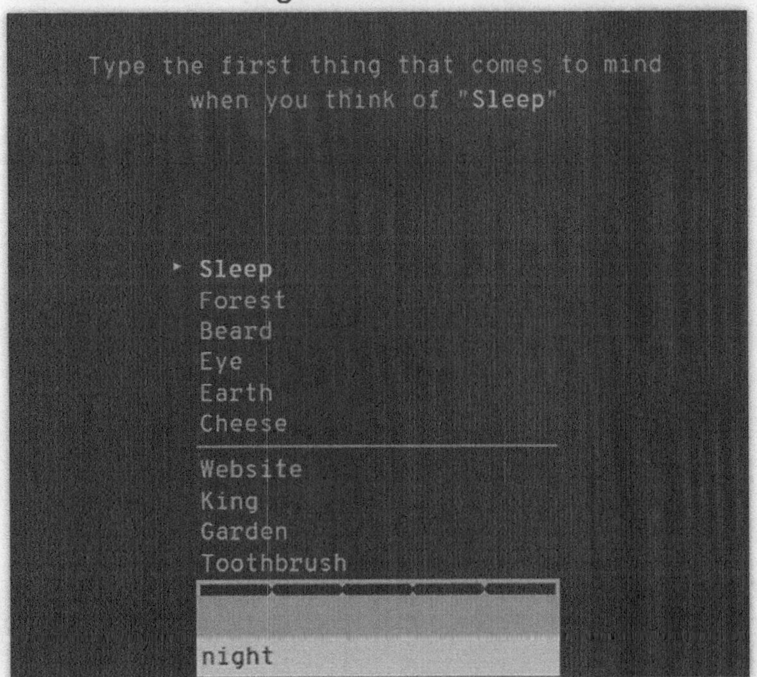

8. So, the word sleep will be highlighted and the adjoining words having the same meaning will be eliminated and you will get the score accordingly.

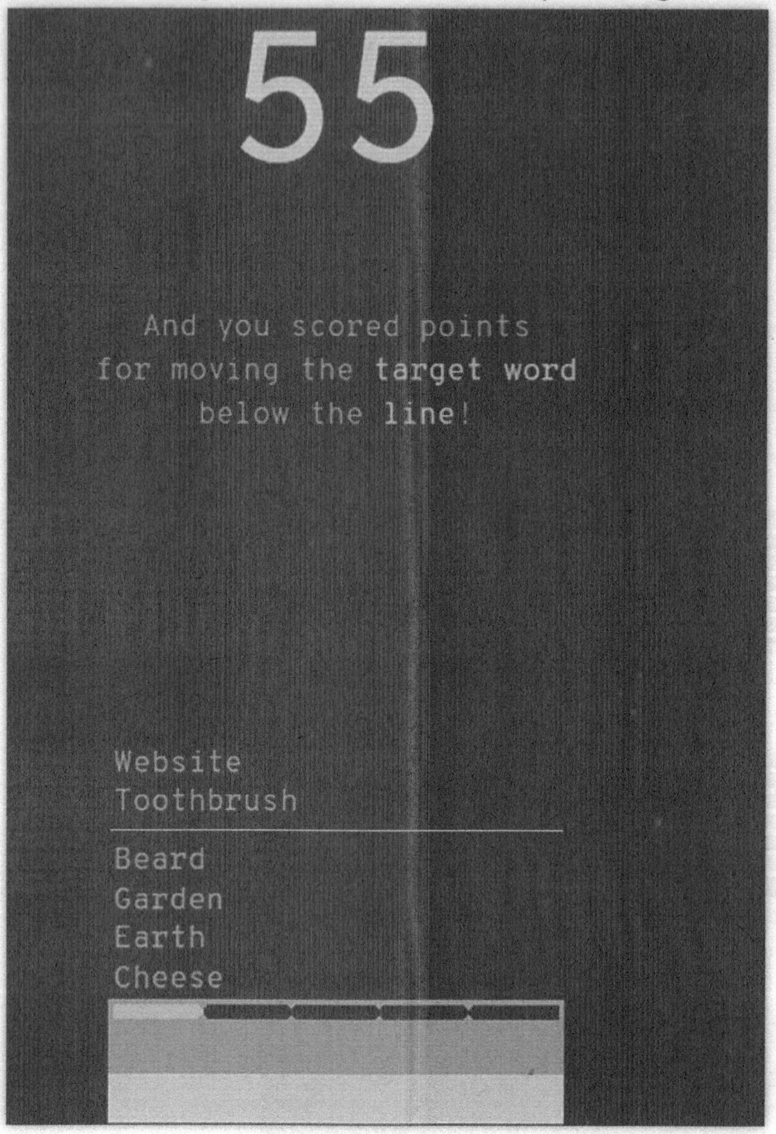

MEMORY BOT

The real-life COG Project was started to explore how AI is affected by real-world experiences.

Tech Bot

- **The state space:** The set of possible situations.
- **Transitions:** Possible moves between one state to another.
- **Costs:** Time/Money required to complete the task

RECAP

- Artificial intelligence (AI) is making a computer which thinks like a human to be able to learn and to have new ideas
- The Tower of Hanoi is a mathematical game or puzzle. It consists of three rods and disks of different sizes, which can slide onto any rod. Initially the disk are arrange in ascending order of size on one rod, the smallest at the top, thus making a conical shape.
- AI is as old as computer science. Long before we had computers, people thought of the possibility of automatic reasoning and intelligence.
- Alan Turing designed a very simple device which can compute anything which is computable and the device is known as the Turing machine. Machine lead Turing to the invention of programmable computers that can be used to carry out different tasks depending on what they were programmed to do.
- To solve games using AI, the concept of a game tree is introduced.
- The different states of the game are represented by nodes in the game tree, which is very similar to the planning problems.
- In real world instead of perfect information, there is a host of unknown possibilities from missing information to deliberate deception.
- The Bayes rule can be expressed in many forms. One of the simplest form to express it is in terms of odds. In this we need to take the odds for something which is happening which we'll call prior odds.
- One of the most useful applications of the Bayes rule is the so-called naive Bayes classifier.
- The Bayes classifier is a machine learning technique which is used to classify objects such as text documents into two or more classes.

Brain Bot

A. MULTIPLE CHOICE QUESTIONS.

1. The set of possible situations is called as:
   - a. The state space ☐
   - b. Transitions ☐
   - c. Costs ☐
   - d. Time ☐
2. Possible moves between one state to another is called as:
   - a. The state space ☐
   - b. Transitions ☐
   - c. Costs ☐
   - d. Time ☐
3. Time/Money required to complete the task is called as:
   - a. The state space ☐
   - b. Transitions ☐
   - c. Costs ☐
   - d. Time ☐
4. To formalize a planning problem, we have use the concept:
   - a. The state space ☐
   - b. Transitions ☐
   - c. Costs ☐
   - d. All of the above ☐
5. Artificial intelligence (AI) is making a computer which thinks like a human to be able to _______ and to have new ideas.
   - a. Learn ☐
   - b. Move ☐
   - c. Speak ☐
   - d. Think ☐

B. FILL IN THE BLANKS.

Hint: Old, Puzzle, broken, search, computable

1. The Tower of Hanoi is a mathematical game or________.
2. AI is as ________ as computer science.
3. Alan Turing designed a very simple device which can compute anything which is___________.
4. According to John McCarthy any element of intelligence can be ________ down into small steps.
5. ________and planning techniques were an area where AI lead to great advances in the 1960s.

C. MATCH THE FOLLOWING.

Column A	Column B
1. The state space	i. Time/Money
2. Transitions	ii. computer which thinks like a human
3. Costs	iii. possible situation
4. Artificial intelligence	iv. Turing machine
5. Alan Turing	v. Possible moves

D. ANSWER THE FOLLOWING QUESTIONS.

1. Define the term Turning Test.

____

____

____

2. What is State space?

____

____

____

3. What is search and planning?

____

____

____

4. What do you mean by Bayes rule/ Bayes formula?

____

____

____

5. Define the term Game tree.

____

____

____

Lab Activity Draw with Artist

Description

Artist is a browser-based web application, which allows you to draw with the help of blocks. It is available on code.org.

To perform an activity:

1. Visit the link: https://code.org/
2. Click on Project, and the following screen appears:

3. Scroll down to start a new project, select Artist.

4. The following screen appears:

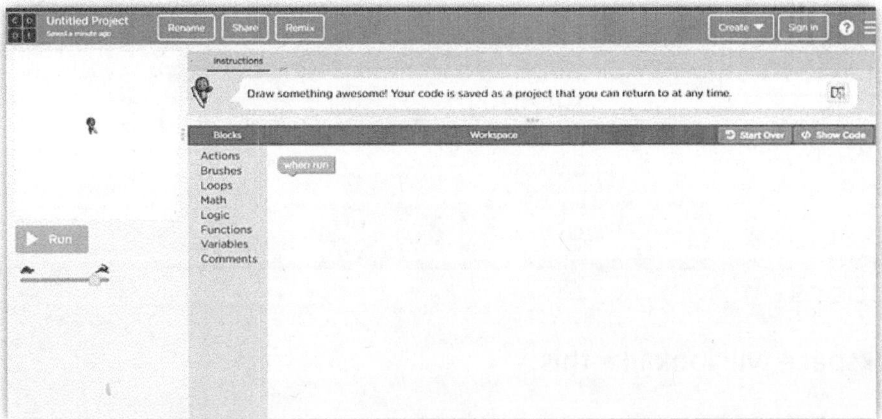

5. In this we are going to draw a hexagon. (Sides of hexagon are 8).

6. In the workspace area,  block is present. You need to add the blocks after this.

7. From Brushes drag the set color block to workspace.

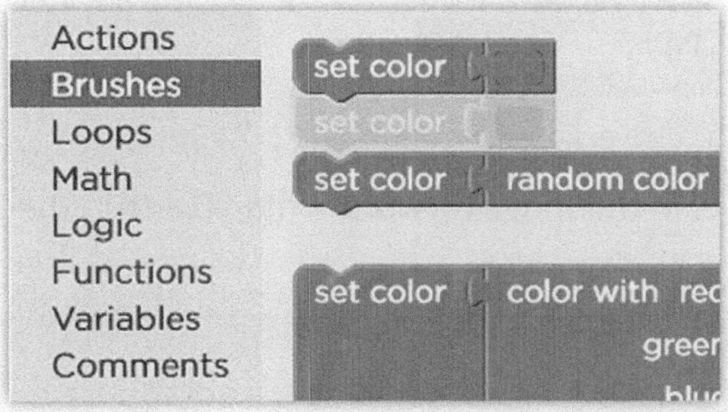

8. From Loop section, select the repeat block, and move it to the workspace.

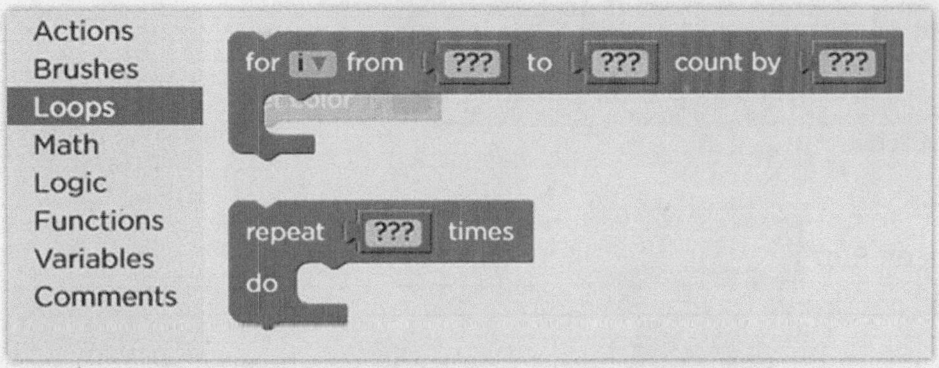

9. From action section, drag move and turn block to workspace.

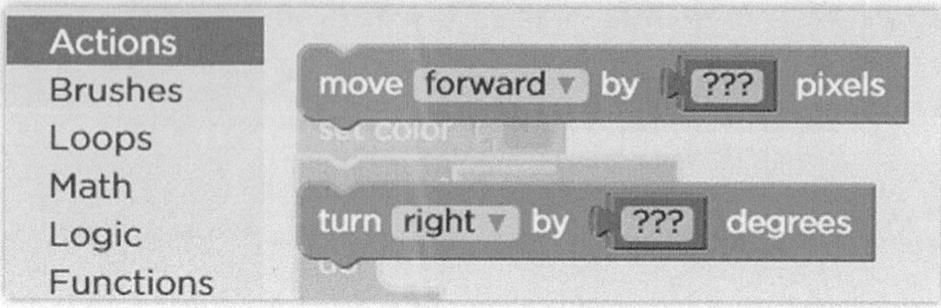

10. The workspace will look like this:

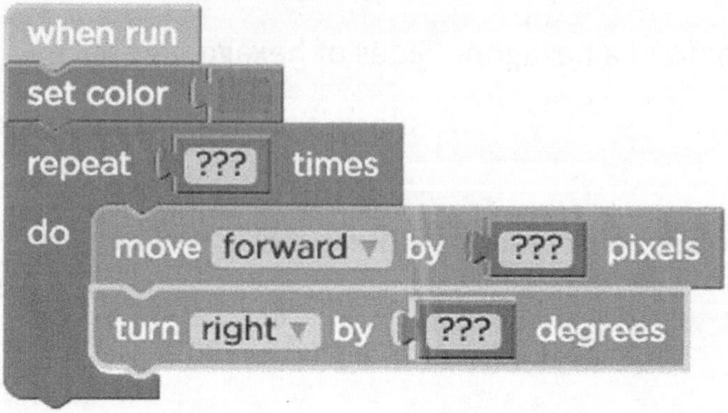

11. In the repeat section, write 8. In the move forward write 60 and in the turn right write 50.

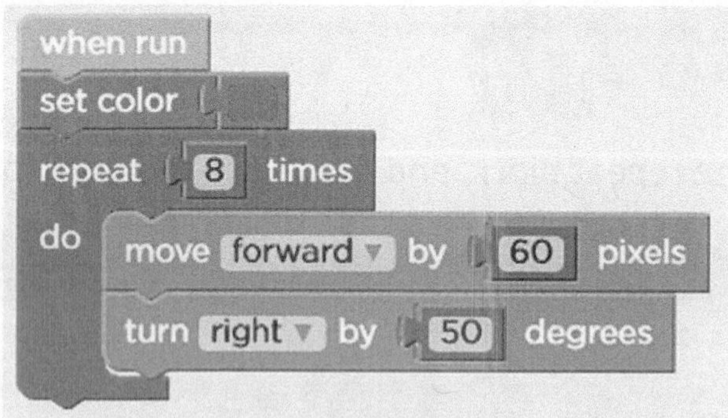

12. Click on Run 

.

13. See the output in the left pane of the window.

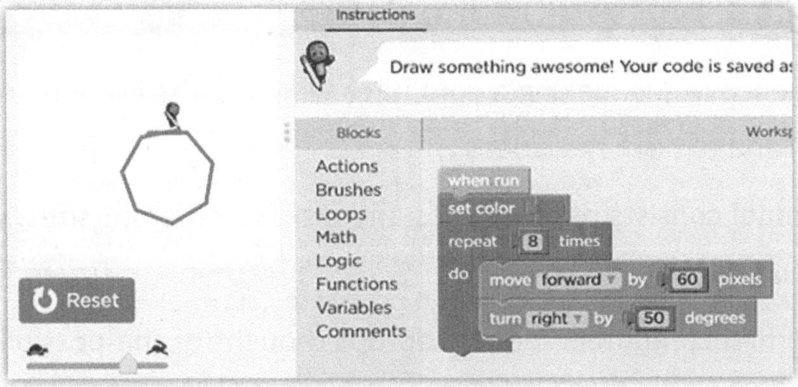

THE TURING TEST

- **Alan Turing** (1912-1954) was an English mathematician and logician.
- He is considered to be the father of computer science.
- He was fascinated by intelligence and thinking, and the possibility of simulating them by machines.
- His most prominent contribution to AI is his imitation game, which later became known as the **Turing test**.

What is Turing Test?

- In the test, a human interrogator interacts with two players, A and B, by exchanging written messages (in a chat).
- If the interrogator cannot determine which player is computer and which is human, the computer is said to pass the test.

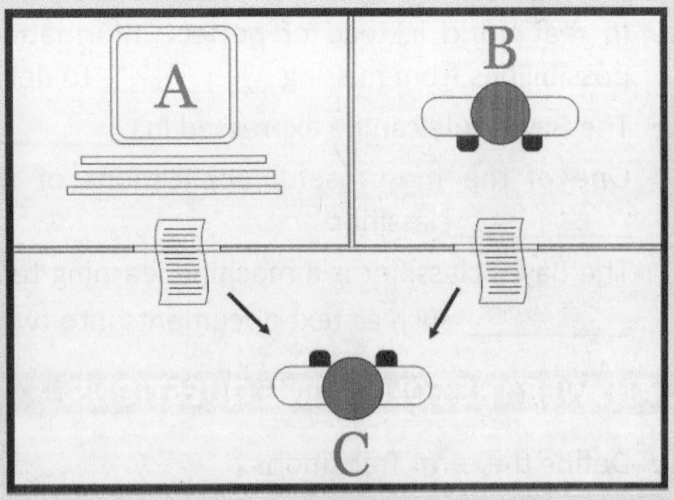

WORKSHEET

A. STATE WHETHER THE FOLLOWING STATEMENT ARE TRUE OR FALSE.

1. Artificial intelligence (AI) is making a computer which thinks like a human to be able to learn and to have new ideas. True / False
2. The Tower of Hanoi consists of three rods and disks of different sizes, which can slide onto any rod. True / False
3. Long before we had computers, people do not thought of the possibility of automatic reasoning and intelligence. True / False
4. Turing machine lead Turing to the invention of programmable computers that can be used to carry out different tasks depending on what they were programmed to do. True / False
5. To solve games using AI, the concept of a game tree is removed. True / False

B. FILL IN THE BLANKS.

Hints: objects, many, information, native Bayes, planning

1. The different states of the game are represented by nodes in the game tree, which is very similar to the __________ problems.
2. In real world instead of perfect information, there is a host of unknown possibilities from missing __________ to deliberate deception.
3. The Bayes rule can be expressed in __________ forms.
4. One of the most useful applications of the Bayes rule is the so-called __________ classifier.
5. The Bayes classifier is a machine learning technique which is used to classify __________ such as text documents into two or more classes.

C. ANSWER THE FOLLOWING QUESTIONS.

1. Define the term Transitions.

____

2. What is the main goal of the state space?

3. Name the term which describe Time/Money required to complete the task.

4. Write any one use of Search and planning techniques.

5. Name the principle way on which Bayes Theorem works.

Quiz Card

TICK THE CORRECT ANSWER.

1. Who is the father of Artificial Intelligence?
   a. Doug Cutting ☐ b. John McCarthy ☐
   c. William S. ☐ d. Rasmus Lerdorf ☐
2. Main goals of AI is:
   a. To Create Expert Systems ☐
   b. To Implement Human Intelligence in Machines ☐
   c. Both a and b ☐ d. None of the Above ☐
3. __________ can contribute to build an intelligent system
   a. Philosophy ☐ b. Biology ☐
   c. Sociology ☐ d. All of the above ☐
4. A computer program with AI can answer the generic questions it is meant to solve.
   a. True ☐ b. False ☐
   c. Ai is not used to answer question ☐
   d. None of the above ☐
5. _________ is not the type of AI.
   a. Reactive machines ☐ b. Unlimited memory ☐
   c. Theory of mind ☐ d. Self-awareness ☐
6. _________ is an application of AI.
   a. Gaming ☐ b. Non-Expert Systems ☐
   c. Non visionary Systems ☐ d. Search system ☐
7. In which university the first demontration of AI program run?
   a. Carnegie Mellon University. ☐ b. Oxford University ☐
   c. Cambridge University ☐ d. Stanford University ☐
8. Expert Ease was developed under the guidance of __________
   a. John McCarthy ☐ b. Donald Michie ☐
   c. Lofti Zadeh ☐ d. Alan Turing ☐
9. Artificial intelligence is about:
   a. Putting your intelligence into Computer ☐
   b. Programming with your own intelligence ☐
   c. Making a Machine intelligent ☐
   d. Playing a Game ☐
10. _____________ is a component of an expert system.
    a. inference engine ☐ b. knowledge base ☐
    c. user interface ☐ d. None of the above

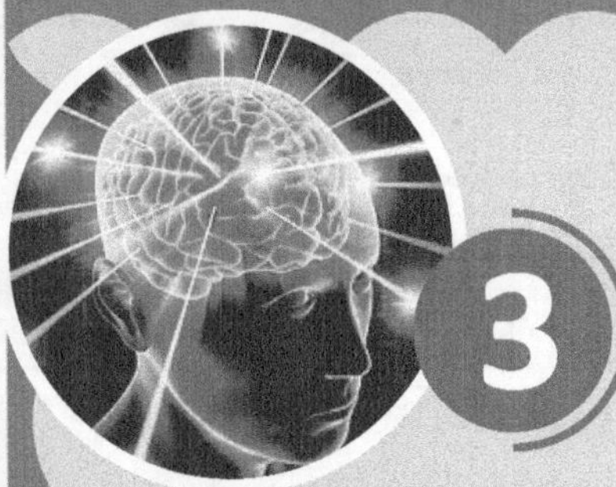

3 MACHINE LEARNING, NEURAL NETWORK AND AI ETHICS

Structure Bot

In this chapter, we will discuss:

- Machine Learning
- Neural Network Basics
- Predicting the future and the societal implications of AI

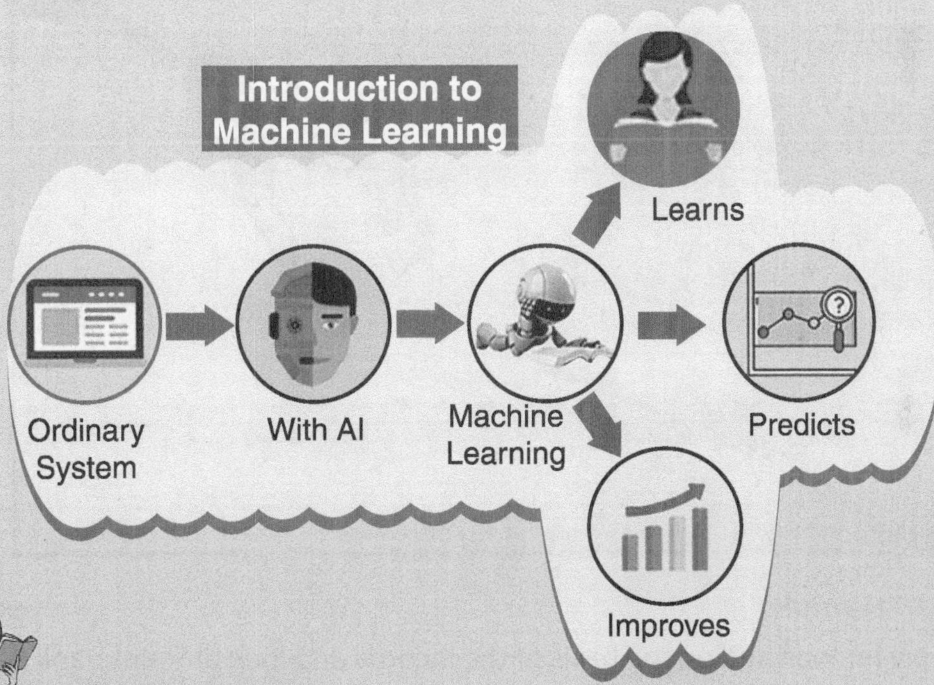

Objective Bot

At the end of this chapter, you should be able to:

- Understand why machine learning techniques are used
- Explain what is neural network
- Know about AI Ethics

Introduction to Machine Learning

Computer process millions of instructions within a second by following the commands given by humans and return the result. It can only perform the task as described by human but cannot take decision by itself.

So, the process of making computer to learn and prepare itself for action is called Machine Learning, Or to make your computer do the task is also known as Machine Learning. In Machine learning we work on data and the property of data points is Features.

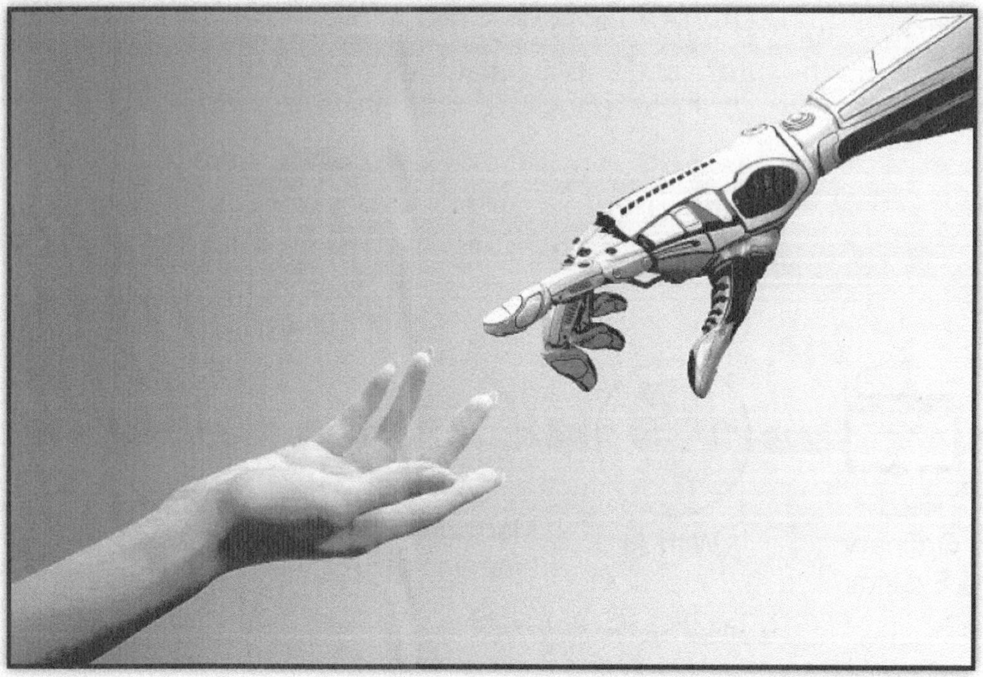

Consider an example:

People apply for loan and on the basis of the income and loan amount bank decides whether to give loan or not. Think, if a person has monthly income of ₹ 10,000/- and applied for the loan of ₹ 3,00,000/- , bank may reject his application early as bank see that he cannot be able to repay it. And if person with ₹ 10,000/- monthly income and applied of loan ₹ 20,000/- then bank may approve its application.

So, based on the past defaulter history, bank creates a data, and this is how the system is train to work.

Fact Bot

Machine learning algorithms are smart algorithms which gives you the power of taking decision on the basis of experience.

Types of Machine Learning

The area of machine learning is divided in subareas according to the kinds of problems being attacked. A rough categorization is as follows:

- **Supervised learning:** We are given an input and the answers to be given in the form of yes/no.

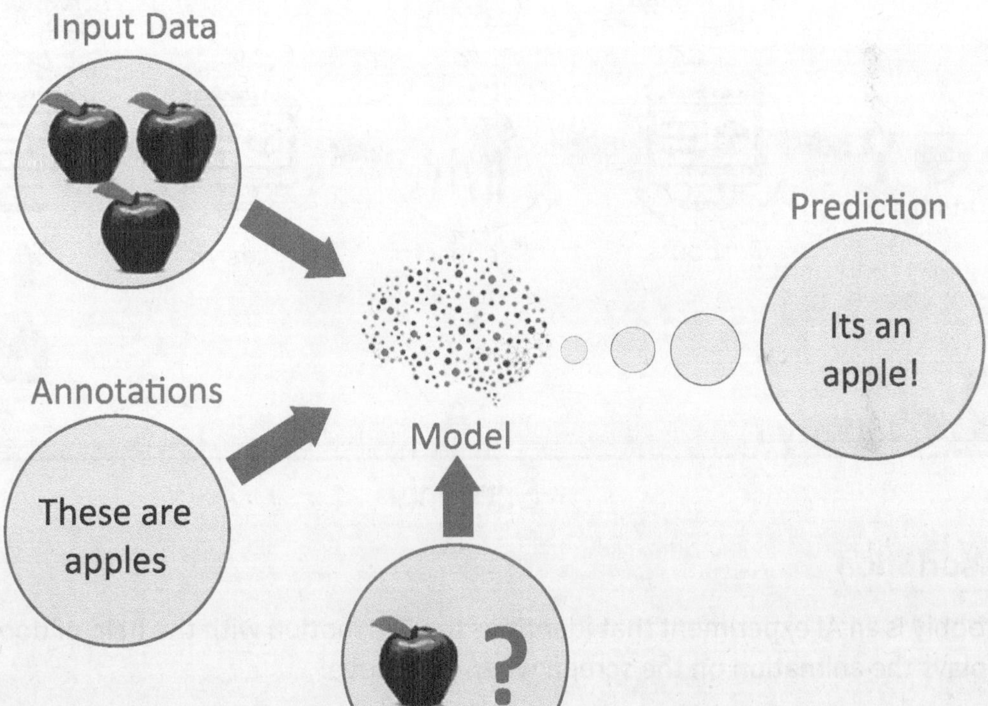

- **Unsupervised learning:** There are no labels or correct outputs. The task is to discover the structure of the data.

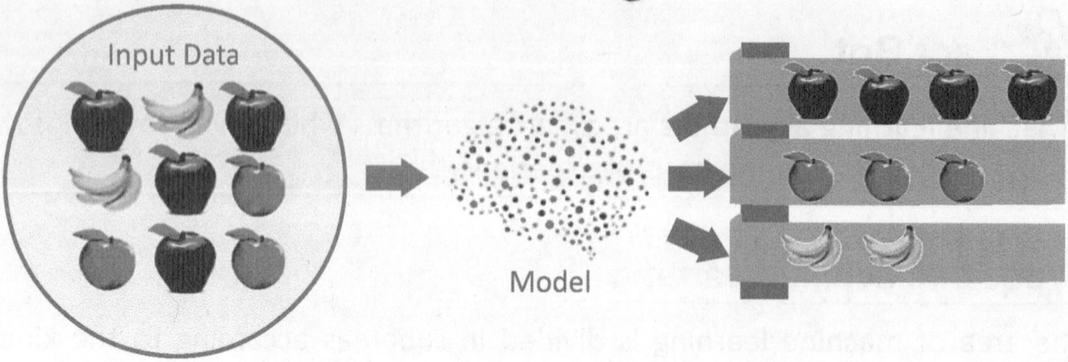

- **Reinforcement learning:** Used in games where the outcome may be decided only at the end of the game.

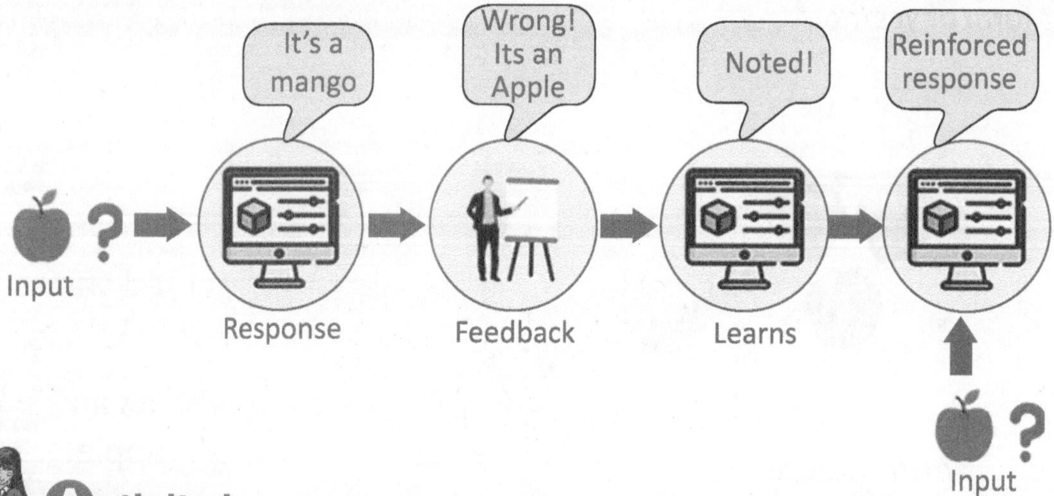

Activity I

Scroobly

Description

Scroobly is an AI experiment that identifies the live motion with the help of doodle and displays the animation on the screen when you move.

Scroobly uses Facemesh and PoseNet machine learning (ML) models to map the live motion to your doodle. The ML system updates the animation seen on screen as you move.

To perform an activity:

1. Go to the link: https://experiments.withgoogle.com/scroobly
2. The following screen appears:

3. Click on LAUNCH EXPERIMENT.
4. Following screen appears, and click on Start:

5. Read the instruction, and click on Next.

6. Click on next again.

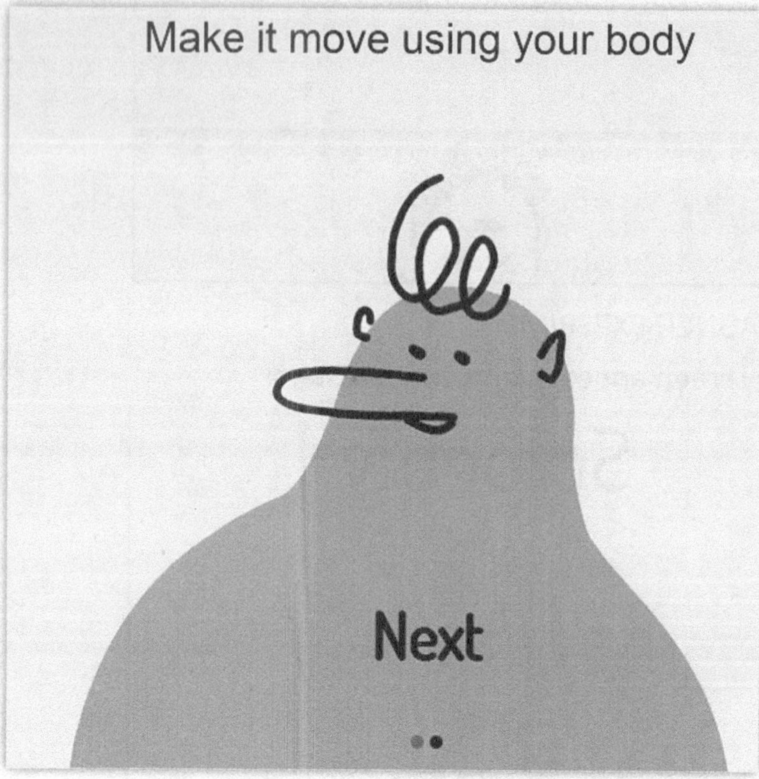

7. Main screen appears, choose a shape and move your body to animate it.

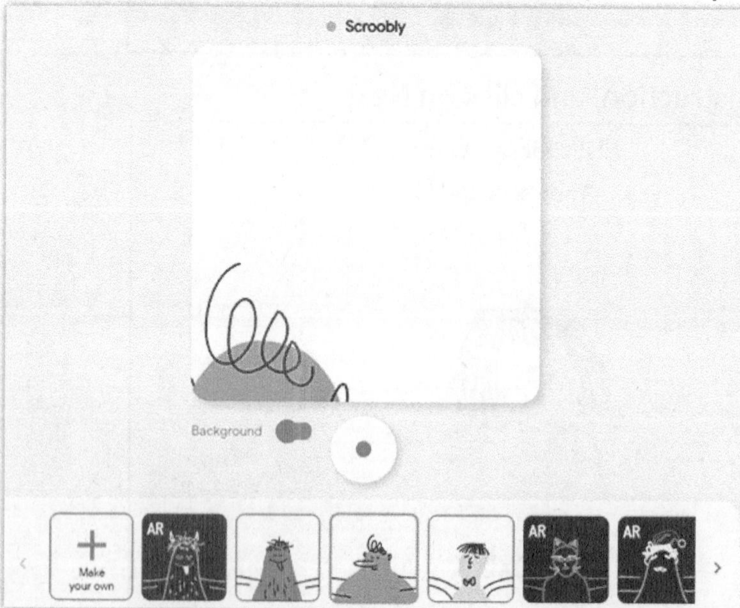

8. You can also turn off the background, to make the background white.

9. Click on the Record button 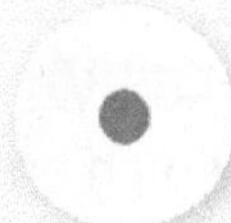 , to record the animation. (Recoding will stop automatically after 15 seconds).

10. To get the doodle animation, click on save.

11. Choose the Export GI, and download the file.

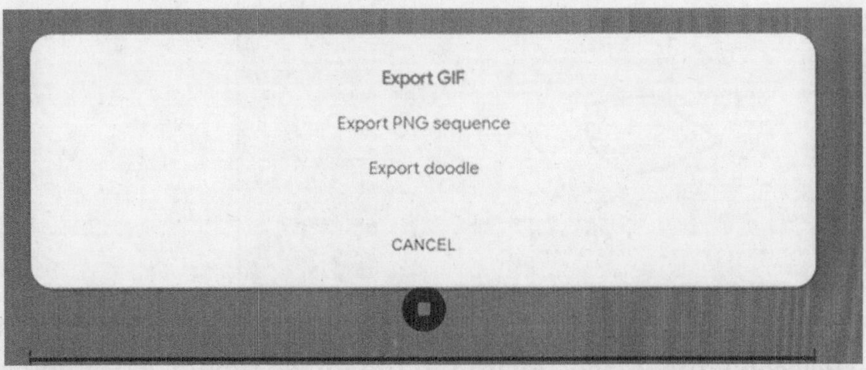

Activity II

Auto draw

Auto Draw is a contemporary drawing tool which employs machine learning or artificial intelligence to transform the rough, horrible sketches, scribbles, and doodles into an innovative, conventional icons. It is entirely free to create anything visually, and it doesn't require anything to download.

To perform an activity:

1. Visit the link: https://www.autodraw.com/
2. The following screen appears:

3. Click on  icon to start drawing.
4. We have drawn the following image:

You can see we have drawn a sort of figure having 4 sides, and once we remove the pen, AutoDraw will show the images related to the image drawn, in **Do you mean** section. You can choose image from **Do you mean** section to complete the drawing.

DEFINITION

Process of making computer to learn and prepare itself for action is called **Machine Learning.**

Activity III

Google Earth

Description

Google Earth application will let you to explore the worldwide satellite image with 3D buildings and lands around the globe.

To perform an activity:

1. Visit the link: https://www.google.com/earth/
2. The following screen appears:

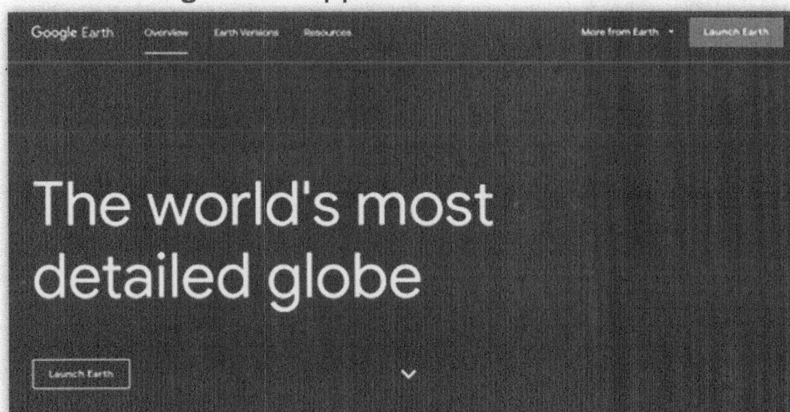

3. Click on LAUNCH EARTH, and the following screen appears:

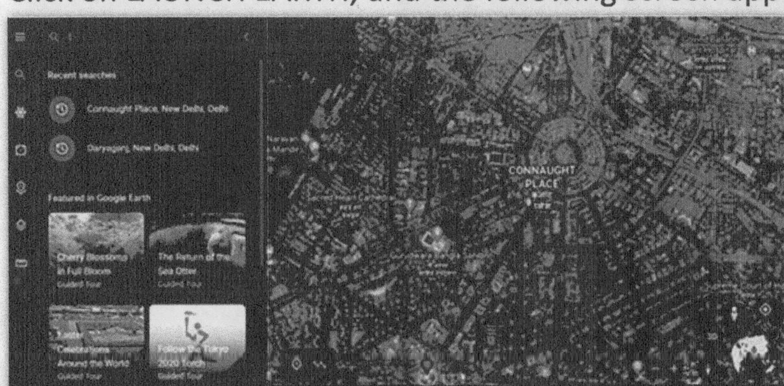

4. To create a story:

a Choose project.

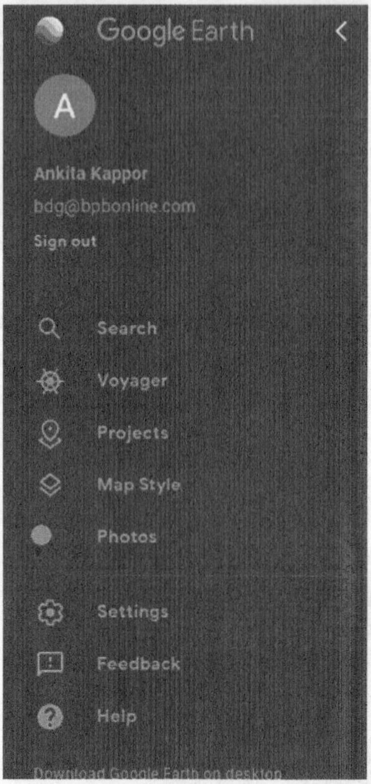

b. Click on create.

c. Choose option, Create a project in Google Drive.

d. Select New feature.

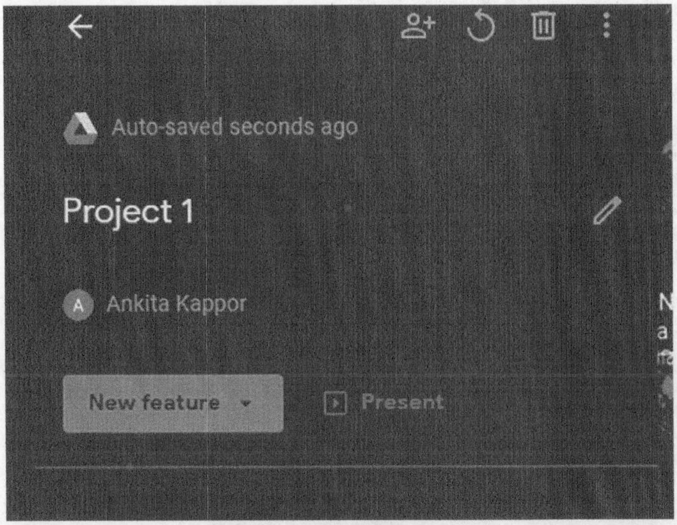

e. Select "Search to add place".

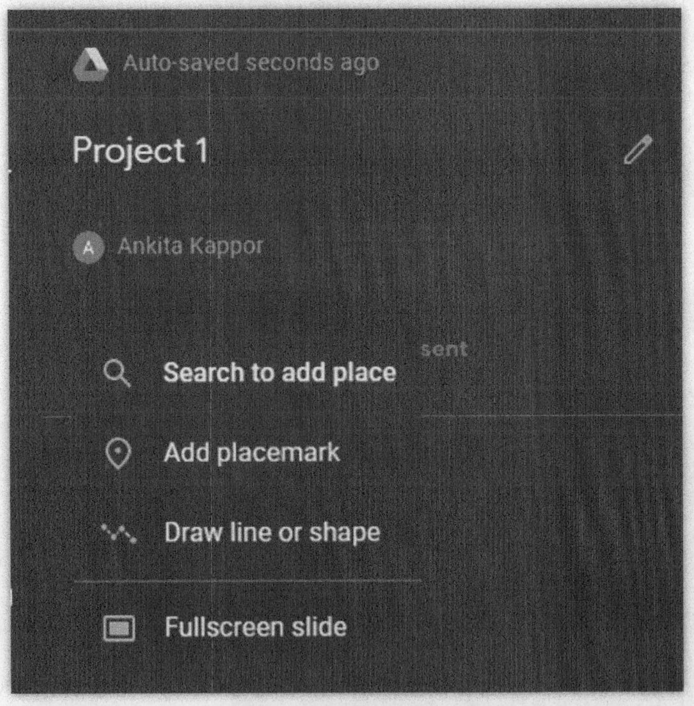

f. The following screen appears:

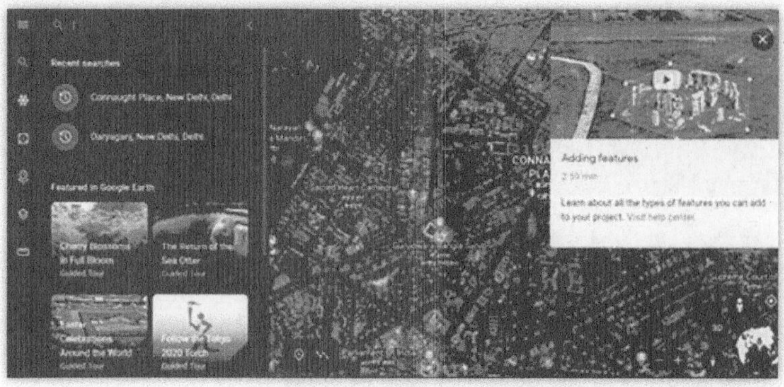

5. Type your destination and click on Add to project.

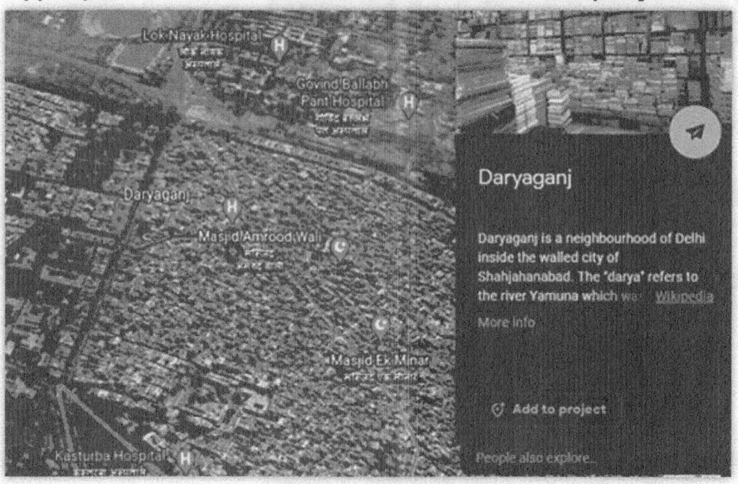

6. Enter the name and click on Save to add it in your project.

7. Similarly, you can add more destinations in the project.
8. Once completed, click on Present to view/show your destination.

9. You can use Previous/Next arrow to go to Previous/Next destination.

Check your Progress - I

State whether the following statements are True or False.

a Computer process millions of within a second by following the commands given by humans and return the result. True / False

b The area of machine learning is divided into subareas according to the kinds of problems being attacked. True / False

c Auto Draw is a contemporary drawing tool which employs Deep learning. True / False

Answer: True, True, False

Neural Networks

A neural network can mean either a "real" biological neural network such as the one in your brain, or an artificial neural network simulated in a computer.

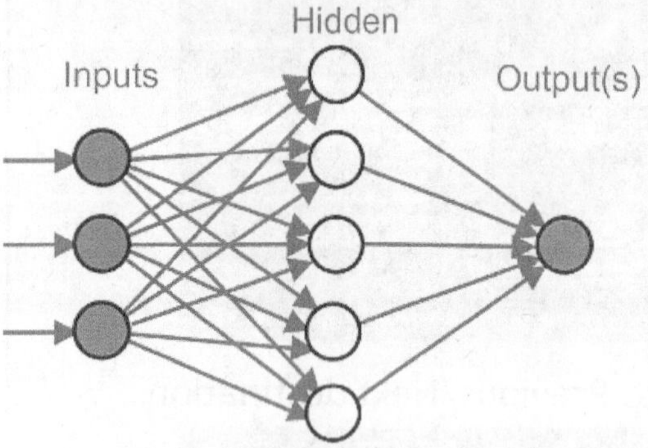

Artificial Neural Network

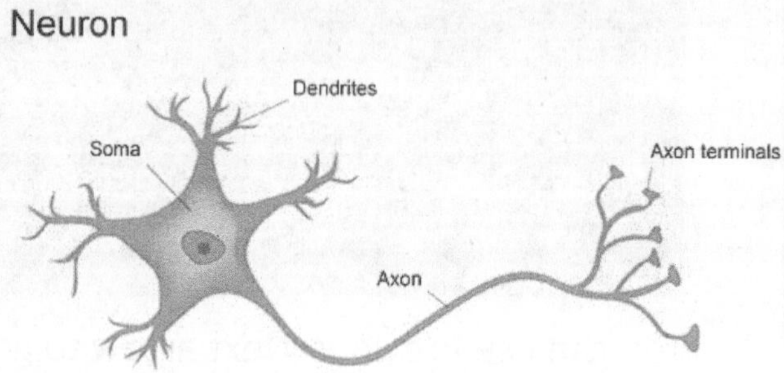

Biological Neural Network

Neurons, cell bodies, signals, dendrites, axon, synapse

- A neural network, either biological or artificial, consists of a large number of simple units, neurons which receive and transmit signals to each other.
- The neurons are very simple processors of information, and it consists of a cell body and wires that connect the neurons to each other.
- Depending on the incoming signals, the neuron may fire and send a signal out for the other neurons to receive.
- Wire that transmits the outgoing signal is called an **axon.**
- Each axon are connected to one or more dendrites at intersections that are called **synapses.**

Tip Bot

Deep learning refers to certain kinds of machine learning techniques where several "layers" of simple processing units are connected in a network.

Activity IV

Run

Description

A game which is based on a musical machine learning algorithm which can generate melodies. The player has to finish the side-scrolling game to listen to the full song.

Instruction

- Use [↑, ←, →] to run and jump!
- Be in the purple band to keep the good vibe!

To perform an activity:

1. Visit the link: http://vibertthio.com/runn/
2. The following screen appears:

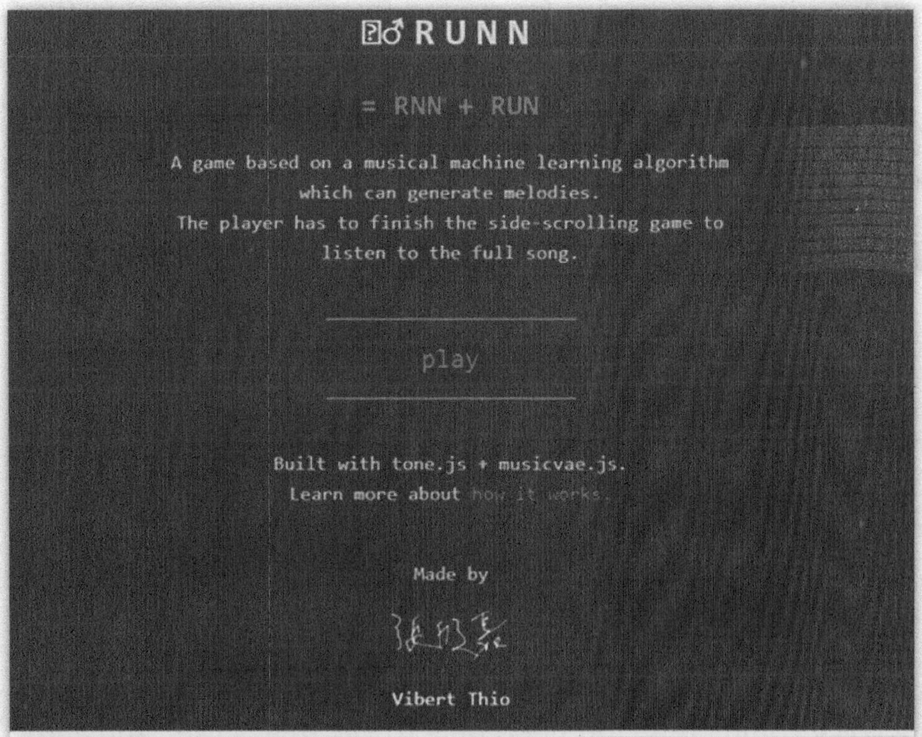

3. Click on play.

4. The following screen appears:

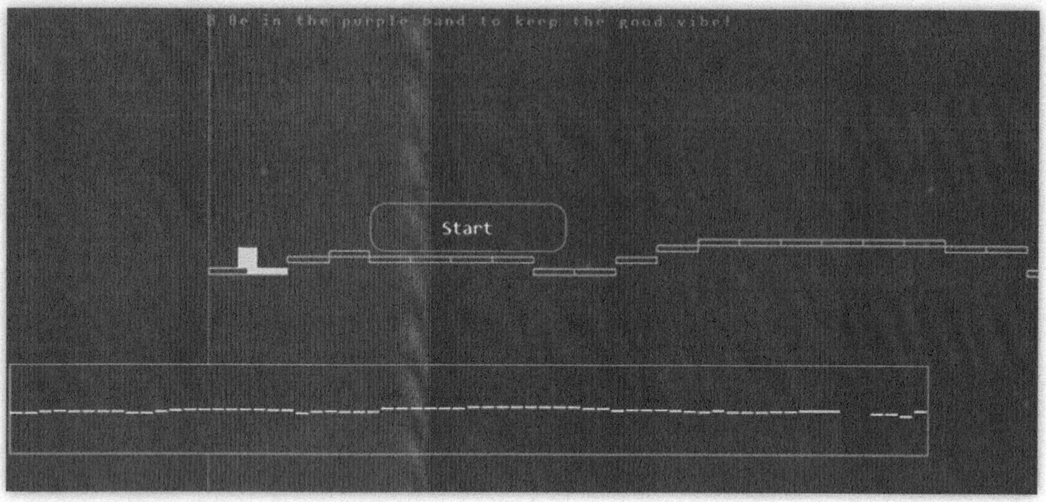

5. Click on Start and play the game.

MEMORY BOT

ML is a part of Artificial Intelligence which learns from the data and provides the results based on the analysis.

DEFINITION

Neural network is either a biological neural network, made up of real biological neurons, or an artificial neural network, for solving artificial intelligence (AI) problems.

Activity V

MixLab

Description

MixLab is an experiment which makes it easier for anyone to create music, by using simple voice commands. You need only to say things like "Add some jazz drums." Or let MixLab surprise you by simply saying "Play me something."

To perform an activity:

1. Visit the link: https://experiments.withgoogle.com/mixlab
2. The following screen appears:

3. Click on LAUNCH EXPERIMENT, and the following screen appears:

4. Click on PREVIEW IT HERE, and speak:

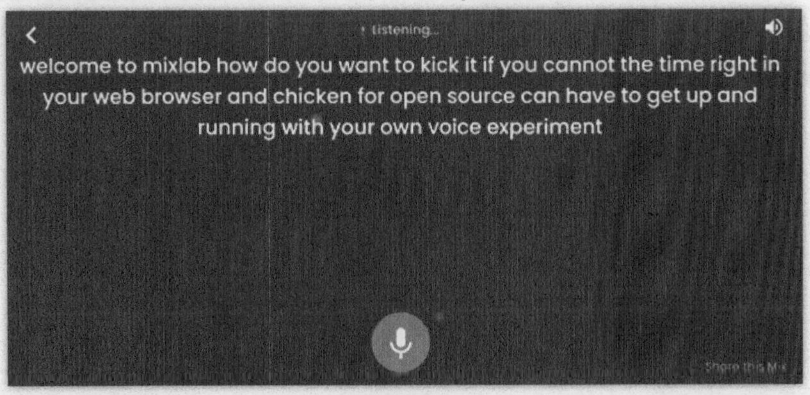

5. It will play a drum beat accordingly.

Fact Bot

The advancement of ML and the involvement of deep learning has created a buzz.

About Predicting the Future

It has also been claimed that AI is a path to world domination. Others make even more extraordinary statements according to which AI marks the end of humanity (in about 20-30 years from now), life itself will be transformed in the "Age of AI", and that AI is a threat to our existence.

Predicting the future is hard but at least we can consider the past and present AI, and by understanding them, hopefully be better prepared for the future, whatever it turns out to be like.

AI winters

The history of AI, has witnessed the coming and going of various different trends. In philosophy of science, the term used for a trend is paradigm. Typically, a particular paradigm is adopted by most of the research community and optimistic predictions about progress in the near-future are provided.

Tip Bot

Poor data representation affects the working of machine learning.

Modern AI

Currently, roughly since the turn of the millennium, AI has been on the rise again. Modern AI methods tend to focus on breaking a problem into a number of smaller, isolated and well-defined problems and solving them one at a time. Modern AI is bypassing grand questions about meaning of intelligence, the mind, and consciousness, and focusing on building practically useful solutions in real-world problems.

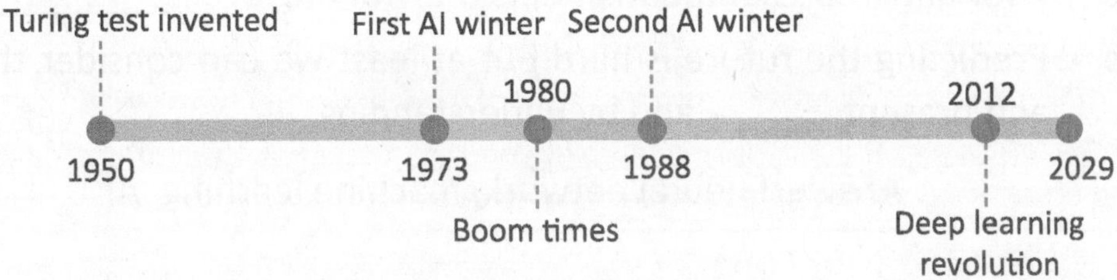

AI making a difference

As a consequence of focusing on practicality rather than the big problems, we live our life surrounded by AI; the music we listen to, the products we buy online, the movies and series we watch, our routes of transportation, and even the news and information that we have available, are all influenced more and more by AI.

MEMORY BOT

Most people create an image of AI in their mind after watching science fiction movies.

Check your Progress - II

Tick the correct option.

Hints: machine learning, AI, neural network

a. A __________ can mean either a "real" biological neural network or an artificial neural network simulated in a computer.

b Poor data representation affects the working of______________.

c Predicting the future is hard but at least we can consider the past and present_______, and by understanding

Answer: neural network, machine learning, AI

The societal implications of AI

AI, and in particular, machine learning, is being used to make important decisions in many sectors.

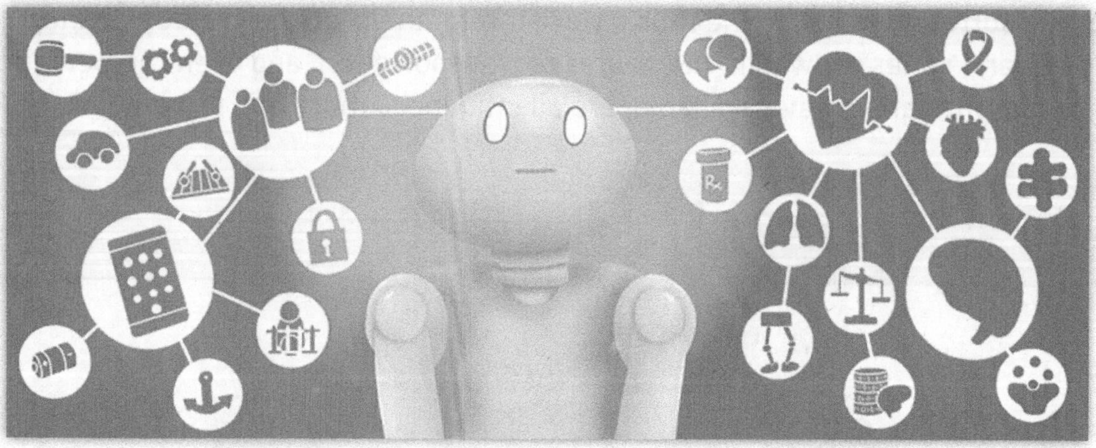

Algorithmic Bias

Consider an example:

A job application filtering tool is trained on the basis of decisions made by humans, In many case the machine learning algorithm may learn to discriminate against women or individuals with a certain ethnic background (if ethnicity or gender are excluded from the data).

So, Algorithmic bias isn't a hypothetical threat, but a real phenomenon which is affecting people today.

Artificial Intelligence already influences several aspects of our society at:

- Consumption habits
- Election results
- Interpersonal relations
- Trade
- Cities
- Culture, law

DEFINITION

Bayes Theorem provides a principled way for calculating a conditional probability.

Online advertising

Online advertisers like Google display ads of lower-pay jobs to the women users as compared to men.

Social networks

Social networks are basing their content recommendations essentially on other users' clicks.

New possibilities which AI is taking to a whole new level

Face2Face: System which is capable of identifying the facial expressions of a person and putting them on another person's face in a Youtube video.

Lyrebird: Tool used for automatic imitation of a person's voice from a few minutes of sample recording.

Activity VI

Introduction to App Lab

App lab is an integrated application of code.org, which helps you to make your own application by using blocks.

To open App Lab:

1. Visit the link: https://studio.code.org/projects
2. The following screen appears:

3. Select App Lab, and the following screen appears:

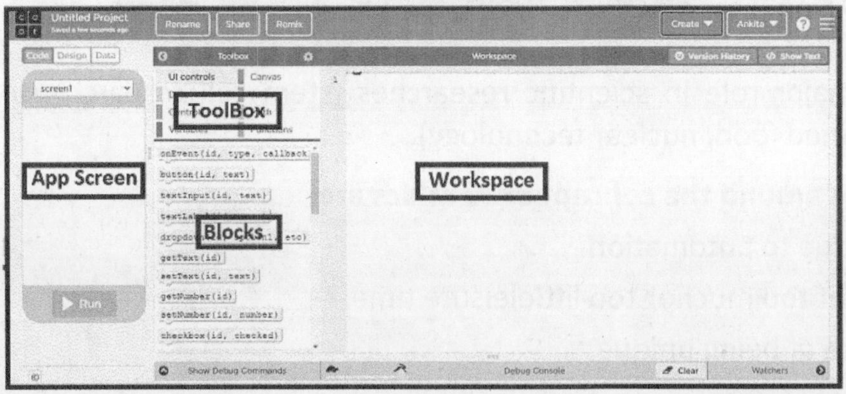

Fact Bot

Autonomous robotics solutions such as self-driving vehicles (cars, drones and boats or ferries) are just at the verge of major commercial applications.

AI Ethics

Artificial Intelligence ethics, or AI ethics, comprise of a set of values, principles, and techniques which employ widely accepted standards of right and wrong to guide moral conduct in the development and deployment of Artificial Intelligence technologies.

Ethics can be defined as:

- The study of values
- Generating moral values for good or bad, right or wrong.

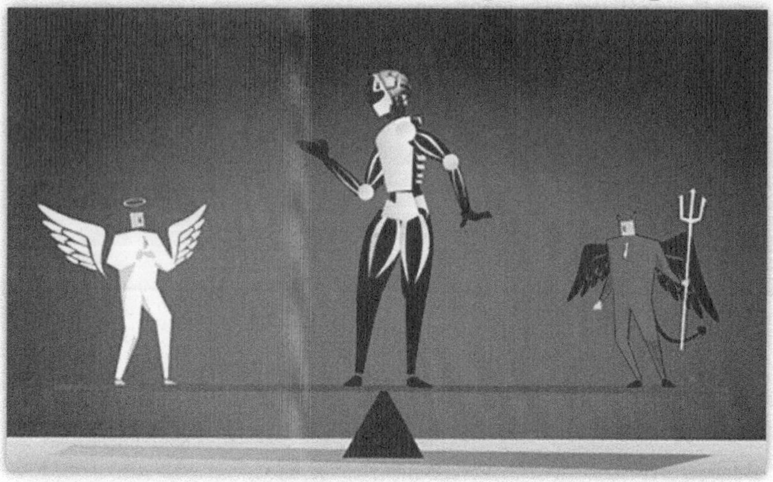

Ethics plays a major role in scientific researches (stem cell research, cloning/ genetically modified food, nuclear technology).

Myths prevailing around the concept of AI ethics are:

- Loss of job due to automation.
- We either get too muchor too littleleisure time.
- Loss of sense of being unique.
- Lose of privacy rights.
- The accomplishment of AI will mean the end of the human race

AI ethics and safety must be a priority in the design and implementation of AI systems. AI Ethics emerges to avoid individual and societal harms which are caused by the misuse, abuse, poor design, or unintended negative consequences of AI systems.

DEFINITION

AI Ethics can be defined as the study of values, generating moral values for good and bad, right, and wrong.

Robot ethics/ Roboethics

Robot ethics can be defined as Morality of how human's constructs, design, use and treat robots and other artificially intelligent created beings.

"Robot rights" is the concept that people must have some moral obligations towards the machines which is created artificially intelligent, similar to human rights or animal rights. Robot rights, such as a right to exist and perform its own mission, can be linked to the robot duty to serve human being, by linking it with human rights to human duties before society.

Robot ethics include:

- Right to life and liberty
- Freedom of thought, expression
- Equality before the law

Threat to Human Dignity

AI technology should never be used to replace the people in the positions which require respect and care. Position which AI cannot or should nor replace humans are:

- A customer service representative (AI technology is currently being used for telephone-based interactive voice response systems)
- A therapist
- A soldier
- A judge
- A police officer

Tip Bot

The neurons are very simple processors of information, and it consists of a cell body and wires that connect the neurons to each other.

Check your Progress - III

Tick the correct option.

a. Ethics does **not plays/plays** a major role in scientific researches (stem cell research, cloning/genetically modified food, nuclear technology).

b. AI ethics and safety **must be/must not** be a priority in the design and implementation of AI systems.

c. Ethics can be defined as the study of **values/subject**, generating moral values for good and bad, right, and wrong.

Answer: plays, must be, values.

MEMORY BOT

AI Ethics and safety must be a priority in the design and implementation of AI system.

Tech Bot

- **Machine Learning:** Process of making computer to learn and prepare itself for action.
- **Neural Network:** A neural network can mean either a "real" biological neural network such as the one in your brain, or an artificial neural network simulated in a computer
- **Face2Face:** System which is capable of identifying the facial expressions of a person and putting them on another person's face in a Youtube video.

RECAP

- Computer process millions of within a second by following the commands given by humans and return the result. It can only perform the task as described by human but cannot take decision by itself.
- The process of making computer to learn and prepare itself for action is called Machine Learning,
- The area of machine learning is divided in subareas according to the kinds of problems being attacked. A rough categorization is as follows:
  - Supervised learning
  - Unsupervised learning
  - Reinforcement learning
- A neural network, either biological or artificial, consists of a large number of simple units, neurons which receive and transmit signals to each other.
- The neurons are very simple processors of information, and it consists of a cell body and wires that connect the neurons to each other.
- Depending on the incoming signals, the neuron may fire and send a signal out for the other neurons to receive.

- Wire that transmits the outgoing signal is called an axon.
- Each axon is connected to one or more dendrites at intersections that are called synapses.
- It has also been claimed that AI is a path to world domination. Others make even more extraordinary statements according to which AI marks the end of humanity (in about 20-30 years from now), life itself will be transformed in the "Age of AI", and that AI is a threat to our existence.
- AI, and in particular, machine learning, is being used to make important decisions in many sectors.
- Artificial Intelligence already influences several aspects of our society at
  - Consumption habits
  - Election results
  - Interpersonal relations
  - Trade
  - Cities
  - Culture, law
- Artificial Intelligence ethics, or AI ethics, comprise of a set of values, principles, and techniques which employ widely accepted standards of right and wrong to guide moral conduct in the development and deployment of Artificial Intelligence technologies.
- Ethics plays a major role in scientific researches (stem cell research, cloning/ genetically modified food, nuclear technology).
- Robot ethics can be defined as Morality of how human's constructs, design, use and treat robots and other artificially intelligent created beings.
- AI technology should never be used to replace the people in the positions which require respect and care.

Brain Bot

A. MULTIPLE CHOICE QUESTIONS.

1. Computer process millions of within a second by following the commands given by:

   a. Humans ☐ b. Pets ☐
   c. Animals ☐ d. Robots ☐

2. Computer can only perform the task as described by ______ but cannot take decision by itself.

   a. Humans ☐ b. Pets ☐
   c. Animals ☐ d. Robots ☐

3. Process of making computer to learn and prepare itself for action is called:

   a. Deep learning ☐ b. Machine Learning ☐
   c. Data ☐ d. Neural network ☐

4. In Machine learning we work on data and the property of data points is:

   a. Information ☐ b. Data model ☐
   c. Features ☐ d. Raw facts or figure ☐

5. _________algorithms are smart algorithms which gives you the power of taking decision on the basis of experience

   a. Deep learning ☐ b. Machine Learning ☐
   c. Data ☐ d. Neural network ☐

B. FILL IN THE BLANKS.

Hint: games, problems, data, labels, yes/no

1. The area of machine learning is divided in subareas according to the kinds of _______ being attacked.
2. In Supervised learning we are given an input and the answers to be given in the form of________.
3. In Unsupervised learning there are no _______ or correct outputs.

4. In Unsupervised Learning the task is to discover the structure of the________.
5. Reinforcement learning used in ________ where the outcome may be decided only at the end of the game.

C. MATCH THE FOLLOWING.

Column A	Column B
1. Scroobly	i. employs machine learning
2. Auto Draw	ii. "real" biological neural network
3. Google Earth	iii. connected to one or more dendrites at intersections
4. Neural network	iv. identifies the live motion with the help of doodle
5. Axon	v. explore the worldwide satellite image with 3D buildings and lands around the globe

D. ANSWER THE FOLLOWING QUESTIONS.

1. Define the term Machine Learning.

____

____

____

2. Name the application where Machine Learning will help you to complete the drawing.

____

____

____

3. What is Neural Network?

____

____

4. What do you mean by AI Ethics?

5. Define the term Synapses.

Lab Activity Create a circle in App Lab

In Activity VI, you have learnt to open App Lab and its interface. In this activity you will learn to create a circle in App Lab.

To perform an activity:

1. Visit the link: https://studio.code.org/projects
2. The following screen appears

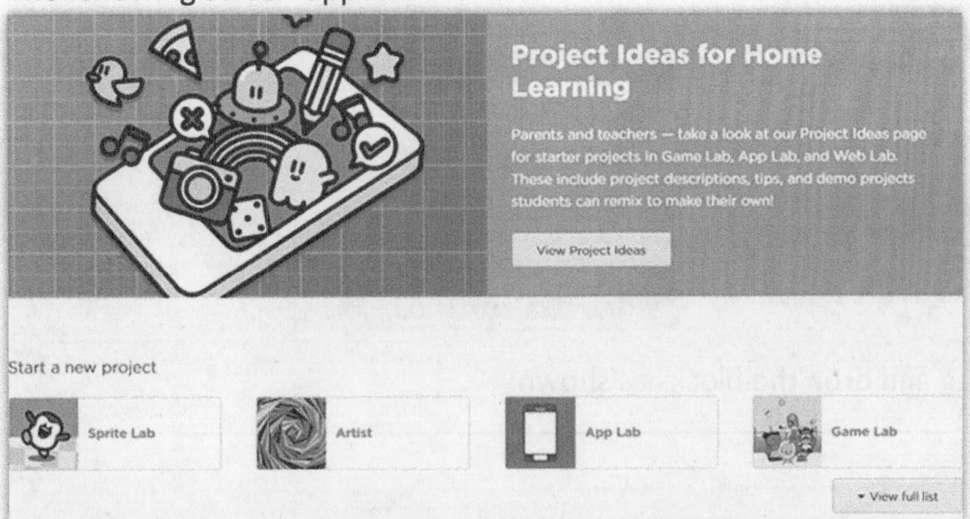

3. Select App Lab, and the following screen appears:

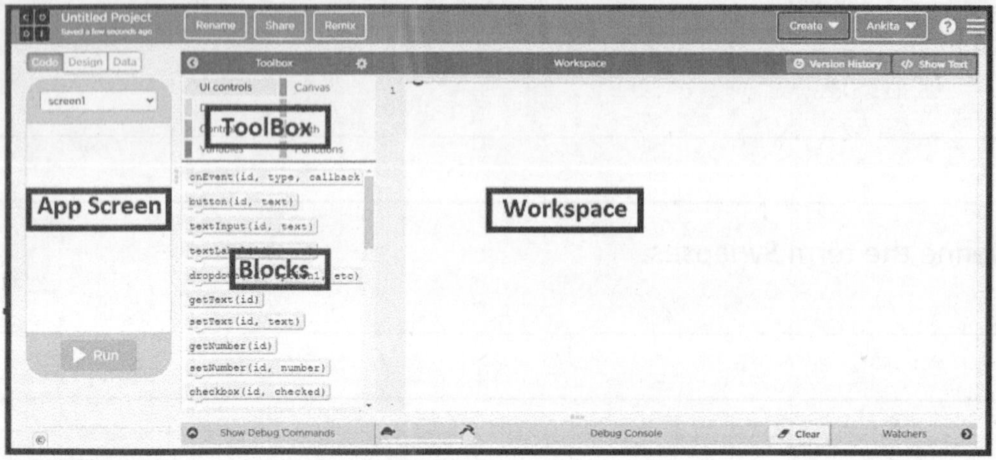

4. Click on Canvas in the toolbox.

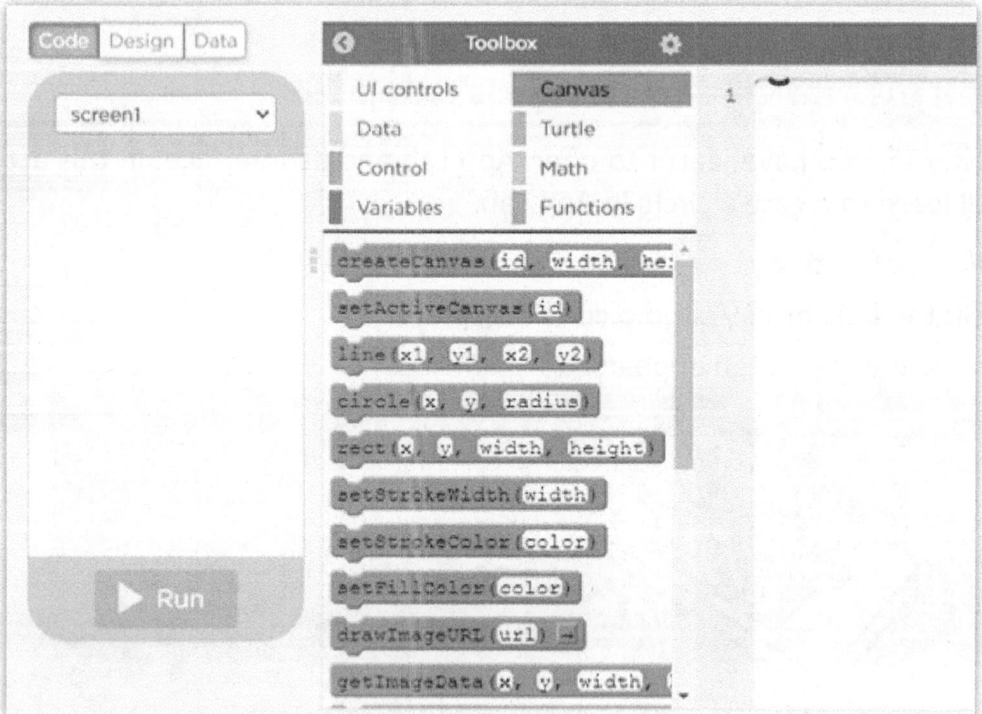

5. Drag and drop the blocks as shown:

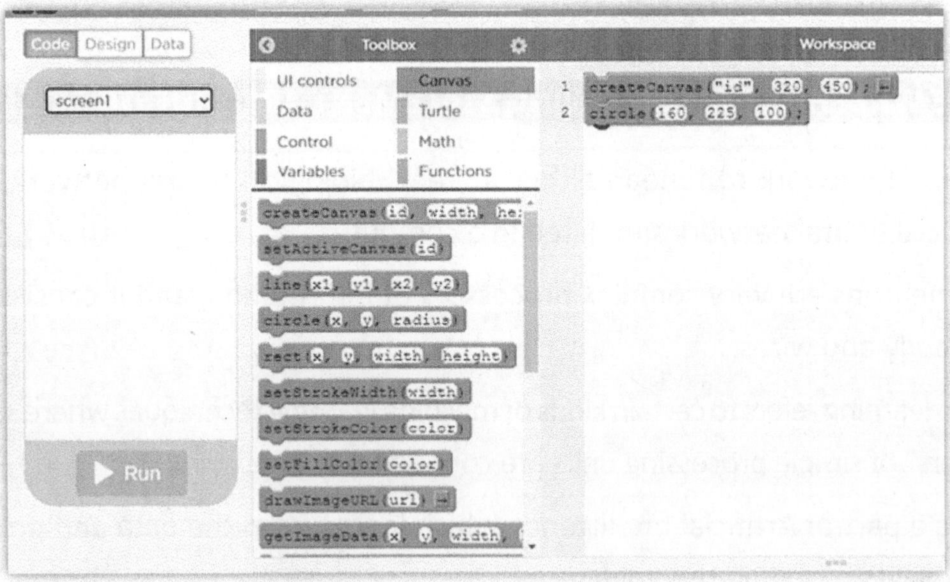

6. Click on Run. 

7. The following output appears:

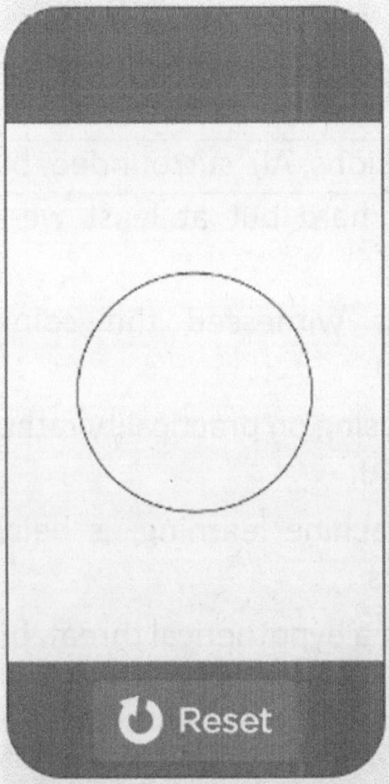

Note: You can run again your project by clicking on Reset 

.

WORKSHEET

A. STATE WHETHER THE FOLLOWING STATEMENT ARE TRUE OR FALSE.

1. A neural network can mean either a "real" biological neural network or an artificial neural network simulated in a computer. True / False
2. The neurons are very complex processors of information, and it consists of a cell body and wires. True / False
3. Deep learning refers to certain kinds of machine learning techniques where several "layers" of simple processing units are connected in a network. True / False
4. ML is a part of Artificial Intelligence which learns from the data and provides the results based on the analysis. True / False
5. The advancement of ML and the involvement of deep learning has created a buzz. True / False

B. FILL IN THE BLANKS.

Hints: decisions, AI, surrounded, bias, trends

1. Predicting the future is hard but at least we can consider the past and present_________.
2. The history of AI, has witnessed the coming and going of various different________.
3. As a consequence of focusing on practicality rather than the big problems, we live our life ________by AI.
4. AI, and in particular, machine learning, is being used to make important ________ in many sectors.
5. Algorithmic _______ isn't a hypothetical threat, but a real phenomenon which is affecting people today.

C. ANSWER THE FOLLOWING QUESTIONS.

1. Name any two areas where Artificial Intelligence influences several aspects of our society .

2. Write any two applications which bring new possibilities to AI and is taking it to a whole new level.

3. Name any three areas where AI Ethics plays an important role.

4. Define the term Robot ethics/ Roboethics.

5. Explain how AI is a threat to human dignity.

Quiz Card

TICK THE CORRECT ANSWER.

1. What is the need of biological neural networks?
   a. to solve tasks ☐ b. to apply heuristic search methods ☐
   c. to make smart human interactive & user friendly system ☐
   d. all of the above ☐
2. Software helps us:
   a. to bring computer more & more closer to user ☐
   b. to solve complex problems ☐
   c. to be task specific ☐ d. to be versatile ☐
3. Human perceive everything as:
   a. Pattern ☐ b. Data ☐
   c. Emotions ☐ d. Information ☐
4. Machine perceive everything as:
   a. Pattern ☐ b. Data ☐
   c. Emotions ☐ d. Information ☐
5. Pattern classification belongs to:
   a. Supervised learning ☐ b. Un supervised learning ☐
   c. Reinforcement learning ☐ d. None of the above ☐
6. Feature mapping belongs to:
   a. Supervised learning ☐ b. Un supervised learning ☐
   c. Reinforcement learning ☐ d. None of the above ☐
7. Example of a unsupervised feature map is:
   a. text recognition ☐ b. voice recognition ☐
   c. image recognition ☐ d. none of the mentioned ☐
8. Artificial Intelligence ethics, or AI ethics, comprise of:
   a. a set of values ☐ b. principles, techniques ☐
   c. accepted standards of right and wrong to guide moral conduct ☐
   d. All of the above ☐
9. AI Ethics plays a major role in:
   a. Scientific researches ☐ b. Mathematical research ☐
   c. Energy area research ☐ d. Material science ☐
10. Myths prevailing around the concept of AI ethics are:
    a. Loss of job due to automation ☐
    b. We either get too much or too little leisure time ☐
    c. Loss of sense of being unique ☐
    d. All of the above ☐

PROJECT

Scratch

Scratch is a programming language which helps you to write programs for animating the objects and to make an environment interactive.

It's an open source software which allows user to create an interactive, animated projects in a visual programming environment.

Downloading Scratch

1. Go to the link: https://scratch.en.uptodown.com/windows/download
2. The following Screen appears:

3. Click on download, and select Windows option.
4. You can see in the bottom of the window, the Scratch software starts downloading.
5. Once the Scratch is downloaded, it will appear on the download folder:
6. Click on the folder to Install the Scratch.
7. Click on Next to run the setup.
8. Once you complete the Setup the following Scratch Screen appears:

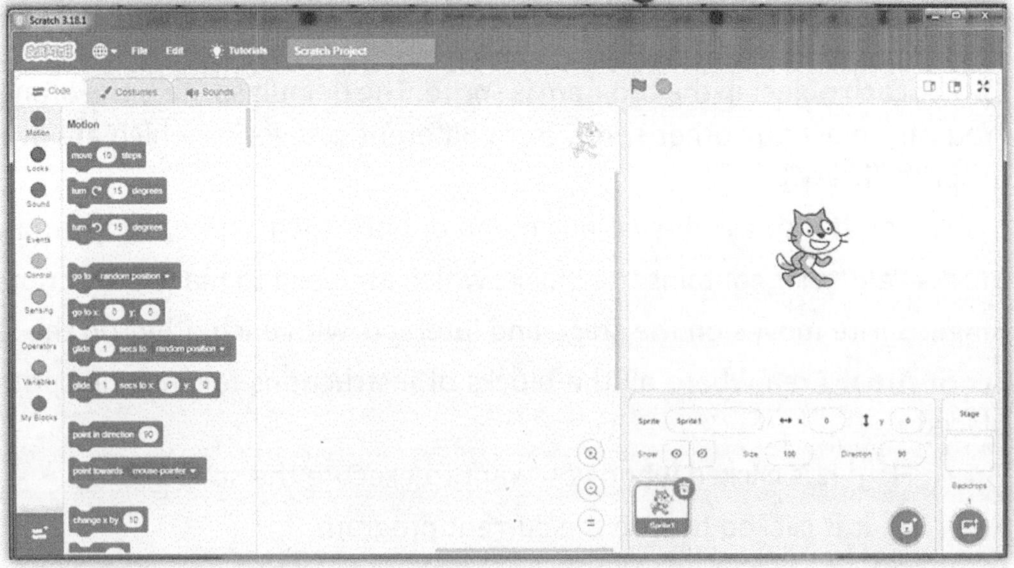

- In Scratch, programs are called SCRIPTS.
- SCRIPT controls an object called a SPRITE.

To start Scratch

1. Click on the Scratch icon present on the screen. 

2. Scratch 3.18.1 window appears:

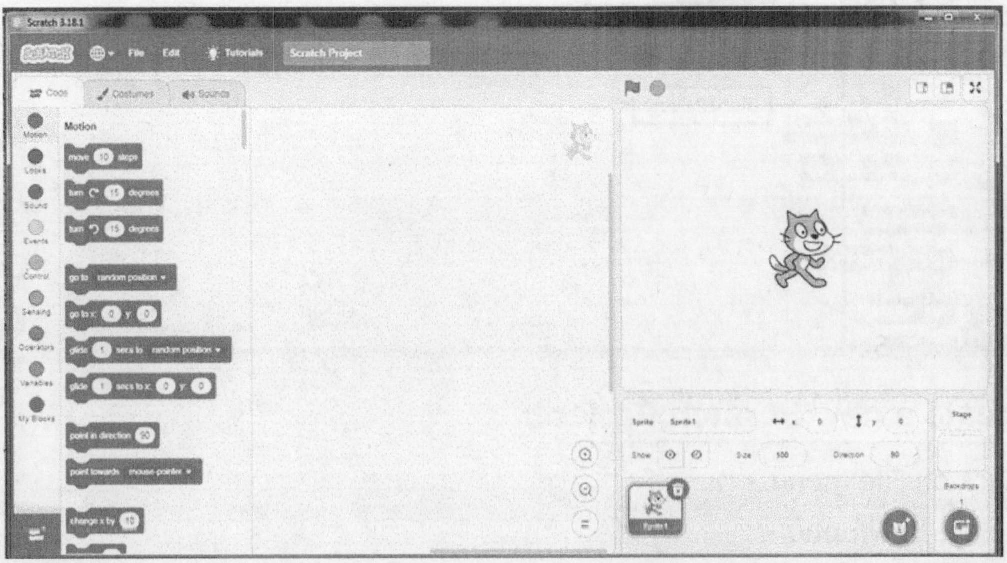

Components of Scratch Window:

1. **Sprite:** Each object in the program is sprite. The default sprite is the orange cat. (You can select any other sprite from different categories which are available in sprite library.)
2. **Menu Bar:** It displays the various menu options such as File, Edit, Tutorial.
3. **Blocks Palette:** It contains the blocks which are used to make our scripts.
4. **Stage:** Sprite moves on the stage and interacts with each other on the stage.
5. **Script Area:** Area where all the blocks of instructions for moving sprites are placed.
6. **Green Flag:** It is clicked when you want to execute the script.
7. **Red Flag:** It is clicked to stop the current program.
8. **Toolbar:** There are four tools to perform an action on sprites, which are Duplicate sprite, Delete sprite, Grow sprite, Shrink Sprite.
9. **Tabs:** It consists of three options: Code, Costumes and Sounds.

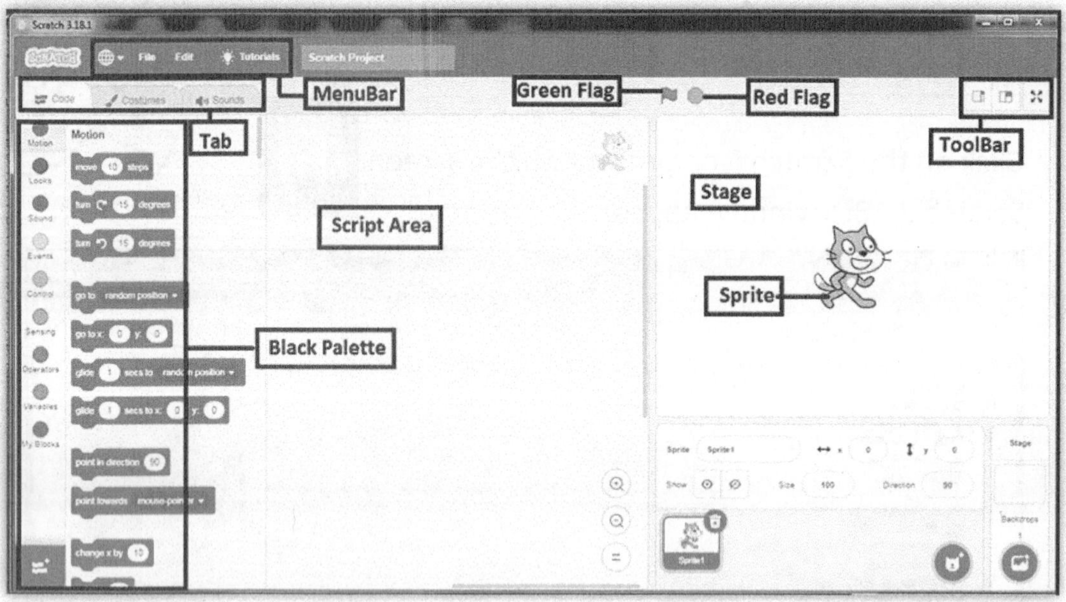

To create a new Scratch Project:

1. Click on File menu.
2. Select New option.

3. A new window will open on the screen.

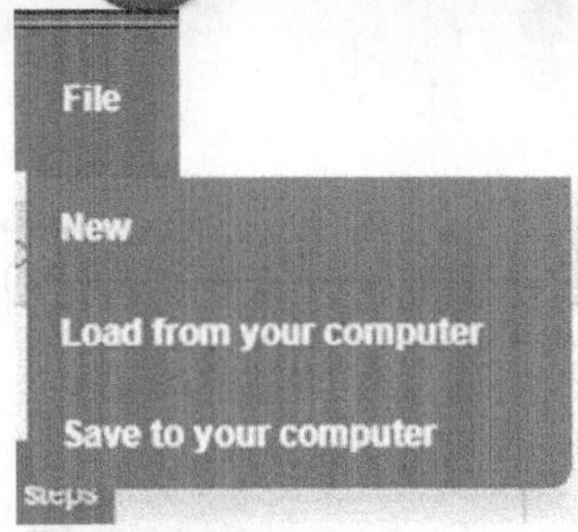

To save a Project:

1. Click on File menu.
2. Choose the save option.
3. The save project dialog box will appear.
4. Select the destination folder where you want to save the file.
5. Type the filename in the text box.

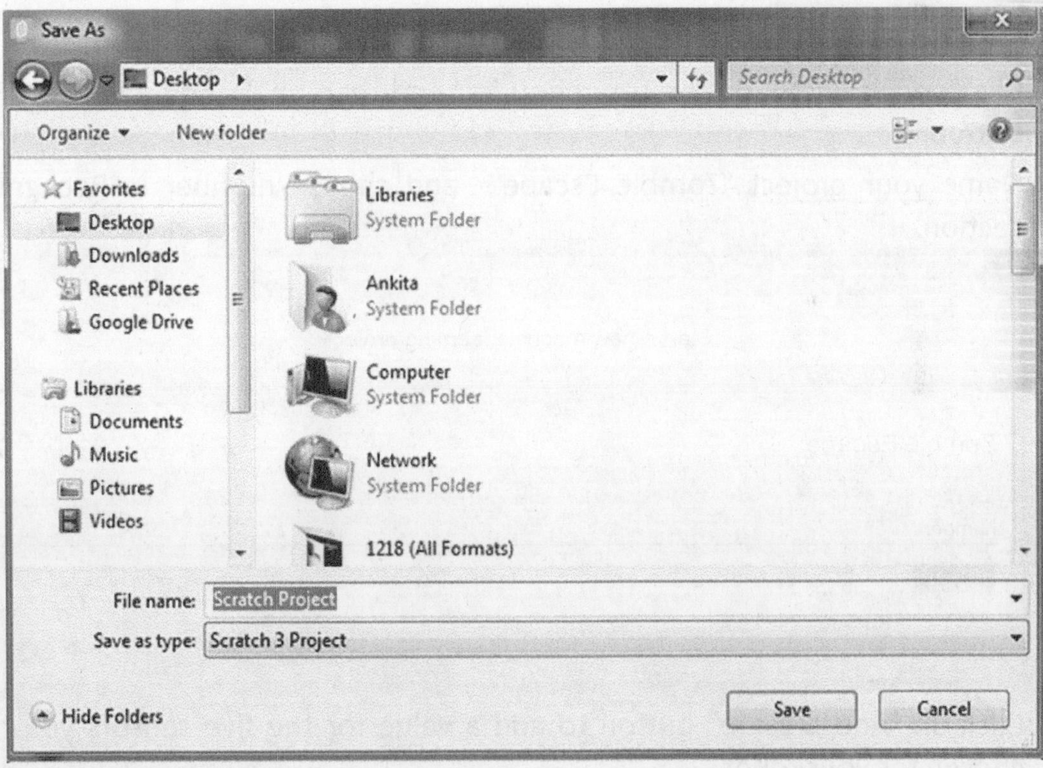

6. Click on Save button.

Extension of scratch file is .sb (scratch project)

Zombie Excape

Description:

- You are trapped in a huge hotel which has been overrun by zombies!
- To escape from the hotel, you have a small remote-controlled robot.
- You need to train your robot to learn the way the zombies behave, and how zombies look like.
- Train your robot to learn which hotel rooms are more likely to be safe, and which rooms you should avoid.

To start project:

1. Go to https://machinelearningforkids.co.uk/.
2. Click on "Get started", and then on "Try it now"
3. Click on "Projects" on the top menu bar and then on "+ Add a new project" button.
4. Name your project "Zombie Escape" and choose number in Recognizing section.

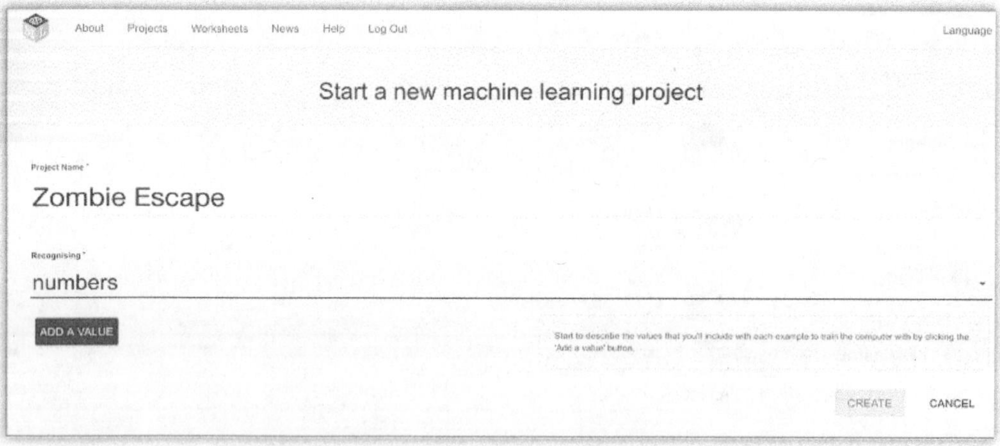

5. Click on "Add a value" button to add a value for the five sensors you have chosen for your robot.

   If you have chosen the **lighting type** sensor, add:

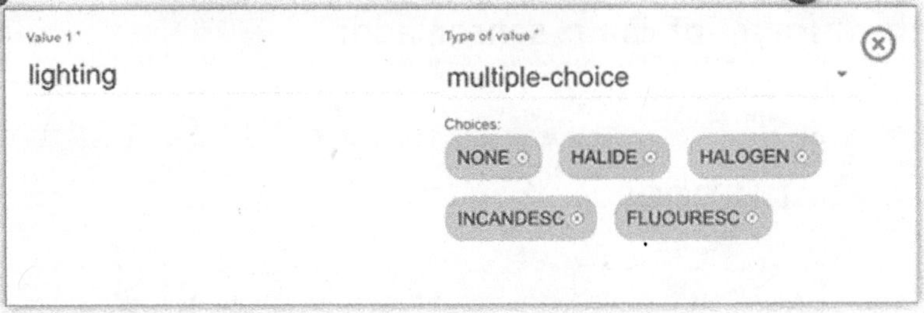

If you have chosen the **temperature** sensor, add:

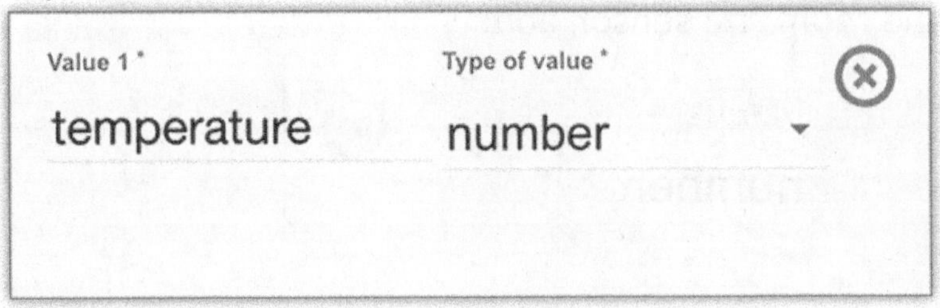

If you have chosen the **floor type** sensor, add:

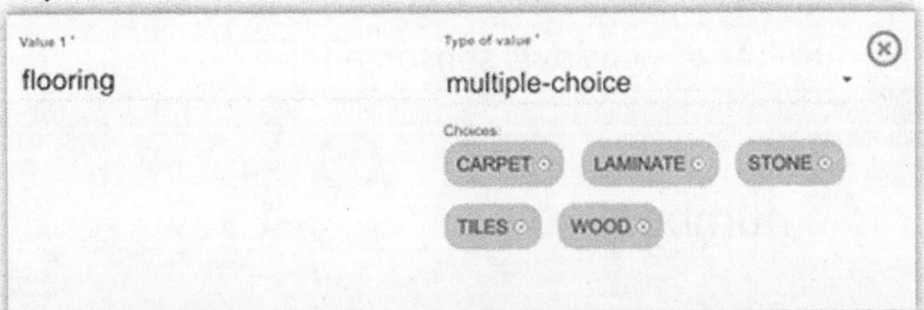

If you have chosen the **humidity** sensor, add:

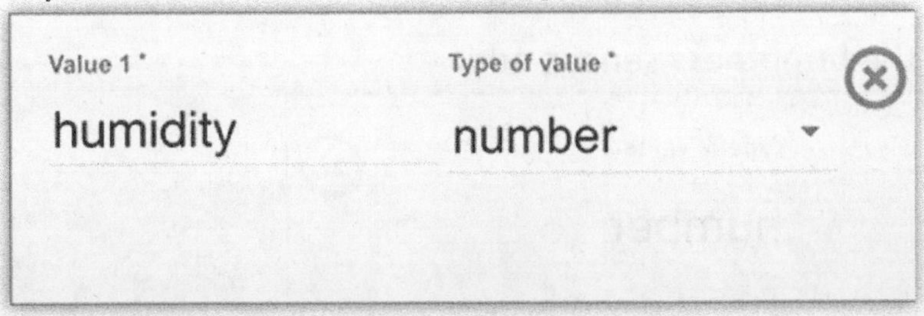

If you have chosen the **wall colour** sensor, add:

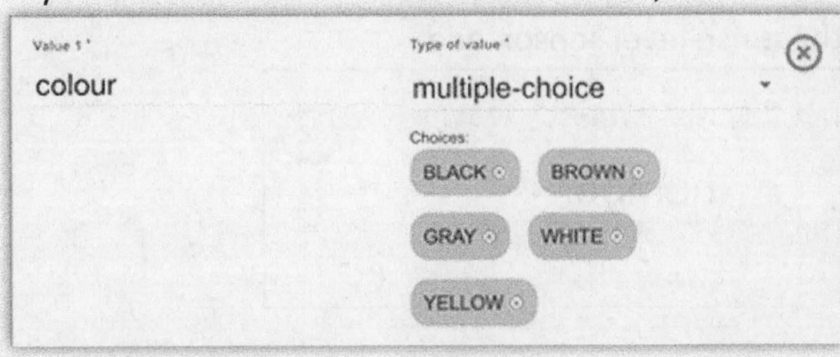

If you have chosen the **number of chairs** sensor, add:

Value 1 *	Type of value *
chairs	number

If you have chosen the **room size** sensor, add:

Value 1 *	Type of value *
room size	number

If you have chosen the **number of windows** sensor, add:

Value 1 *	Type of value *
windows	number

If you have chosen the **brightness** sensor, add:

Value 1 *	Type of value *
brightness	number

If you have chosen the **noise level** sensor, add:

Value 1 *	Type of value *
noise	number

If you have chosen the **number of mirrors** sensor, add:

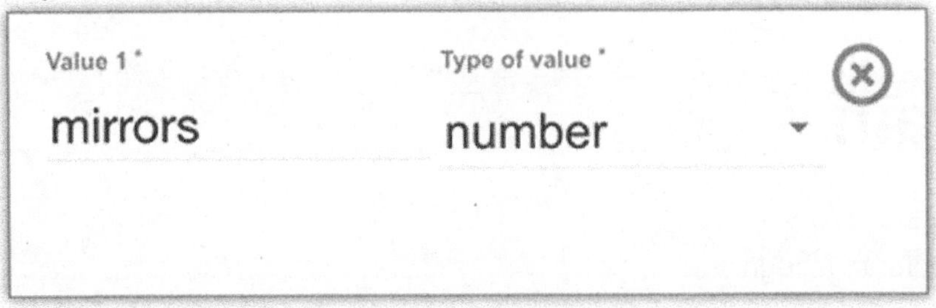

If you have chosen the **room number** sensor, add:

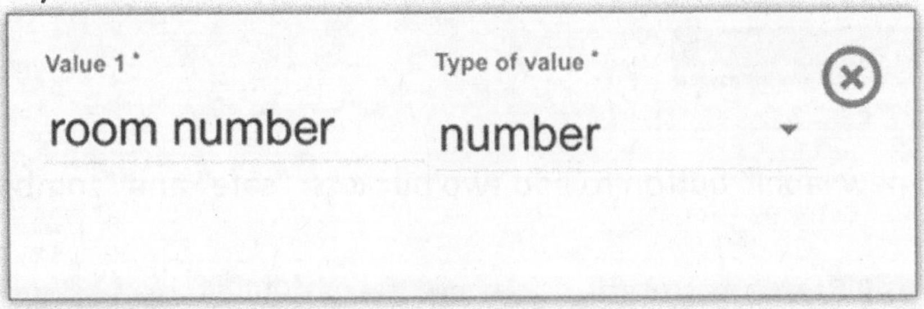

6. When you choose any five sensors, your screen will look like:

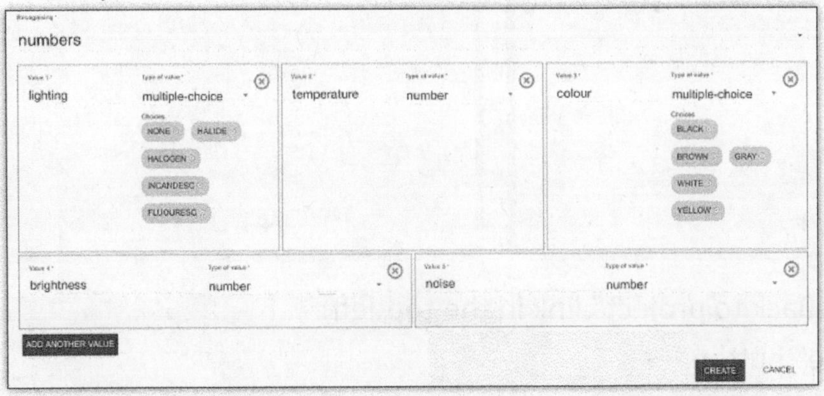

7. Click on "Create".
8. Zombie Escape appears in your list of projects. Click on it.

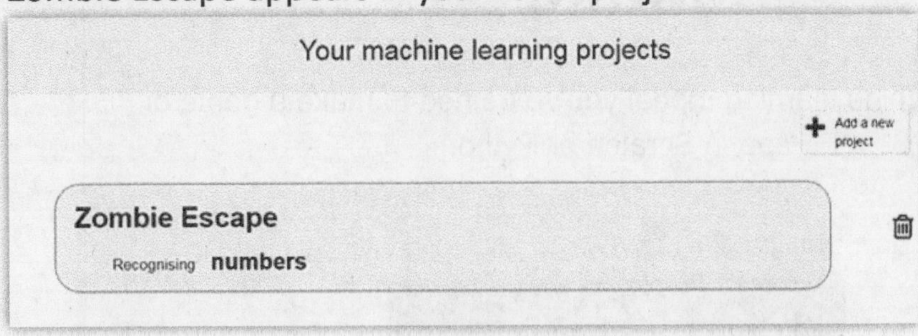

9. Click on "Train"

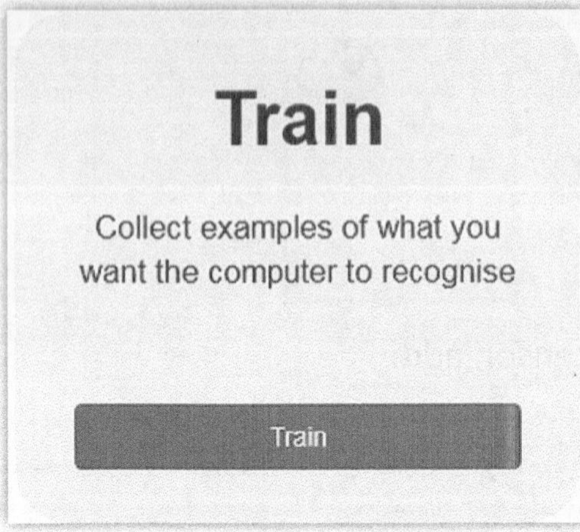

10. Click on "+ Add new label" button to add two buckets: "safe" and "zombie".

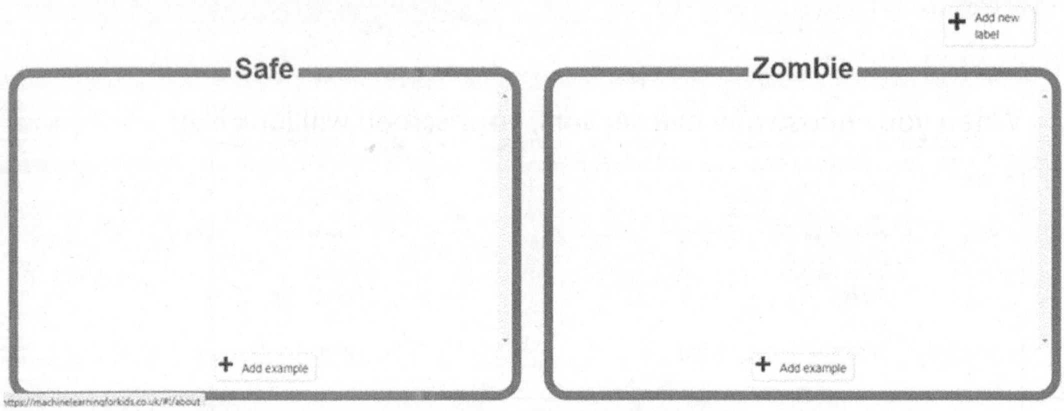

11. Click on the "< Back to project" link in the top-left.
12. Click the "Make" button

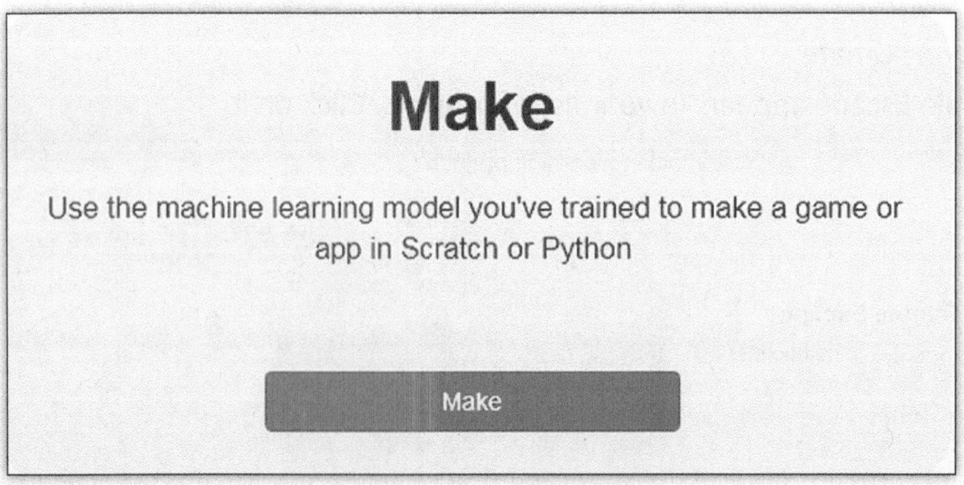

13. Click on "Scratch 3".

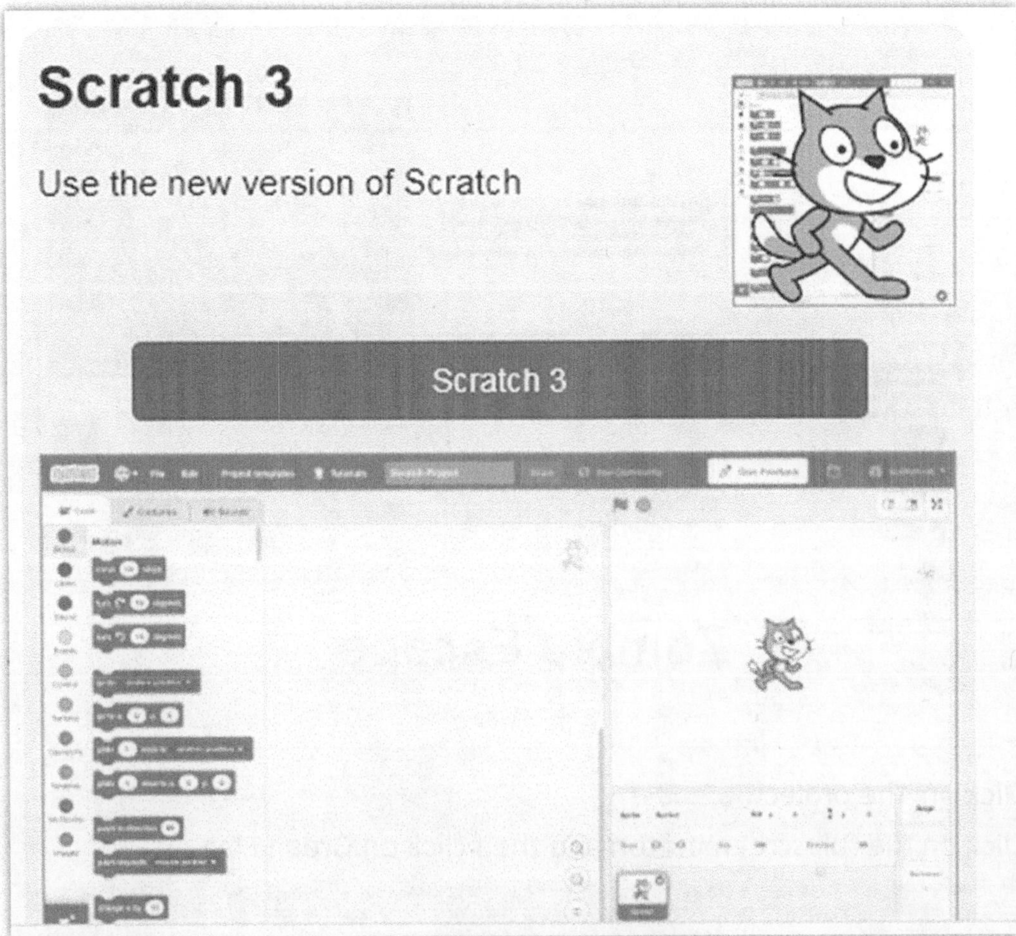

14. Click on "Open in Scratch 3" 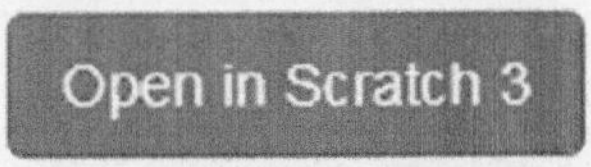

.

15. Click on "Project templates" in the top menu.

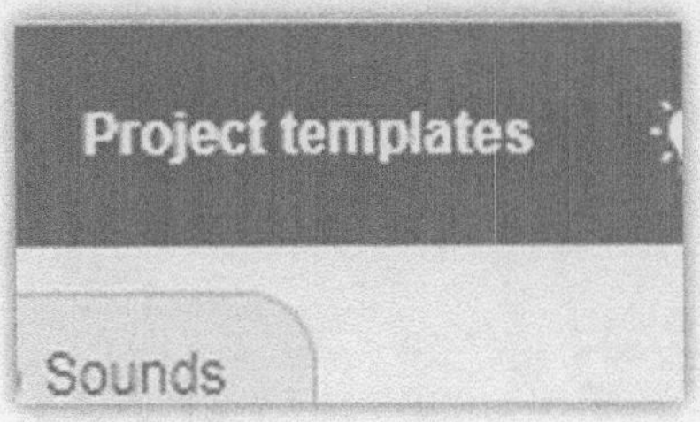

16. Click on the Zombie Escape project template.

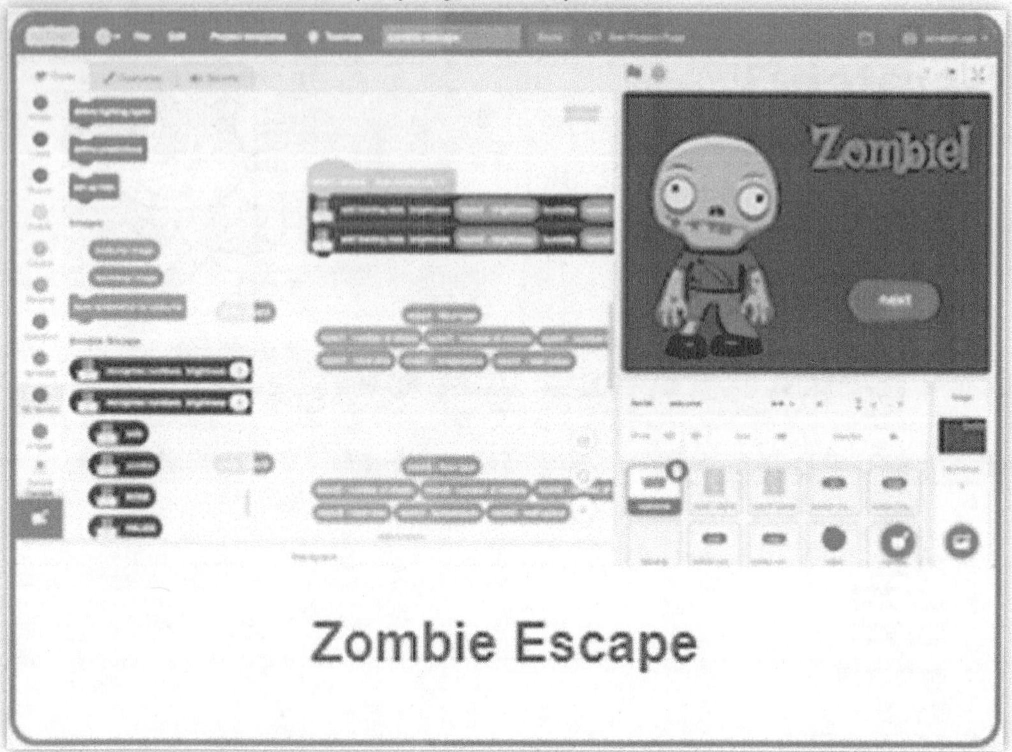

17. Click on the project.

Click on the full-screen button and then click on Green Flag.

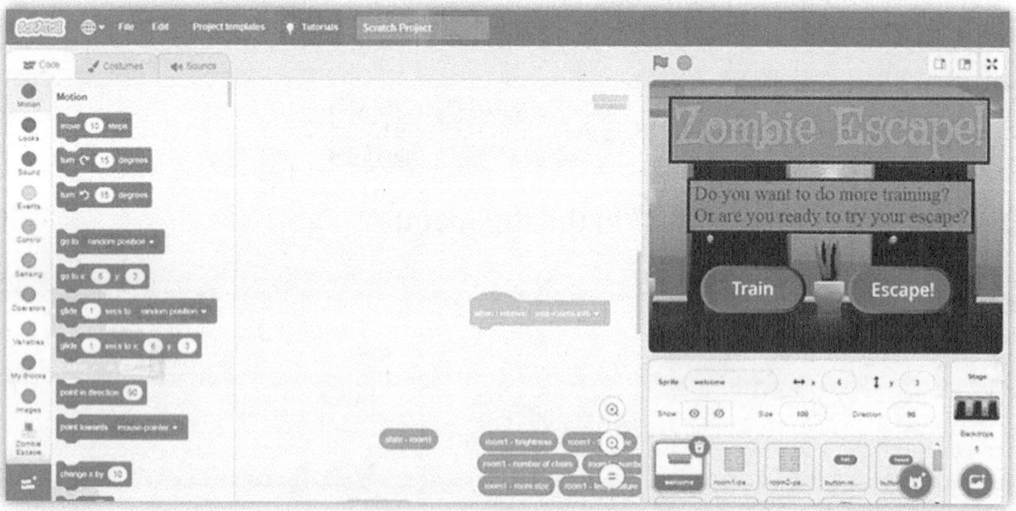

- Click the Train button in the project, the following screen appears:

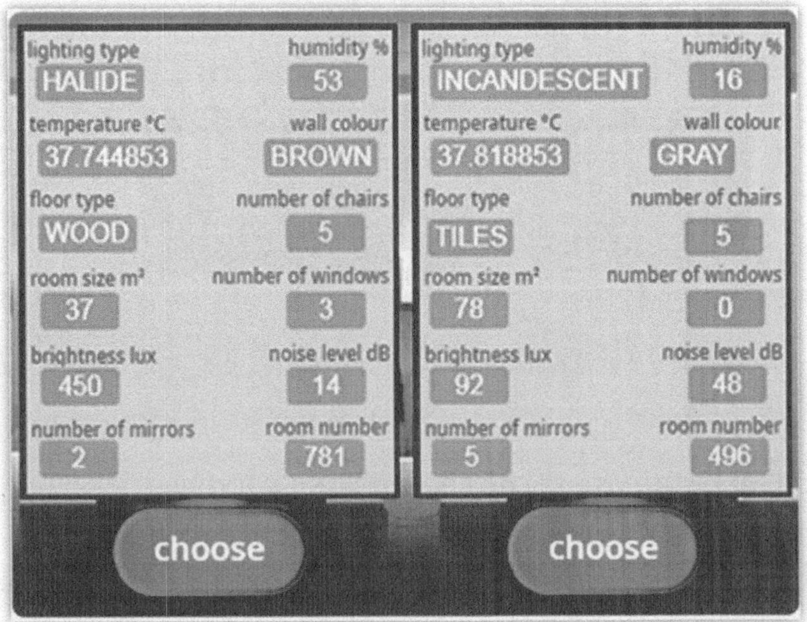

- Each time your robot reaches the doors for the next rooms, it will display it's sensor reading.

- Choose the room you think is probably the safest.
- If you choose correctly, your robot will move on to the next corridor.

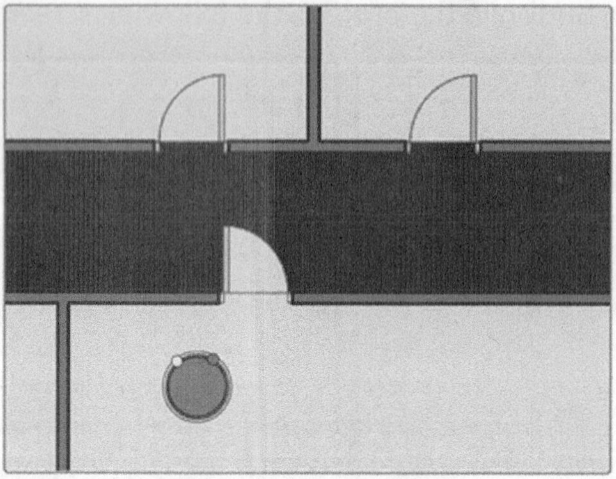

- If you make the wrong choice, you'll see a zombie!

18. Click the "welcome" sprite and find the pink define blocks.

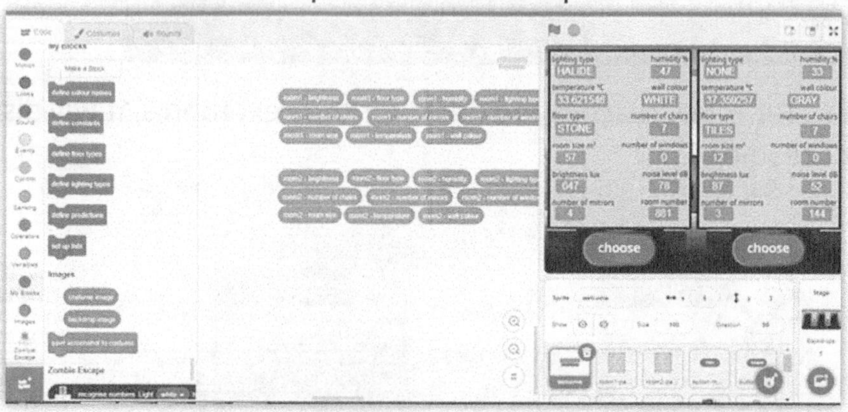

19. Find the define predictions script, and then drag the blocks with the names of your two training buckets into the script.

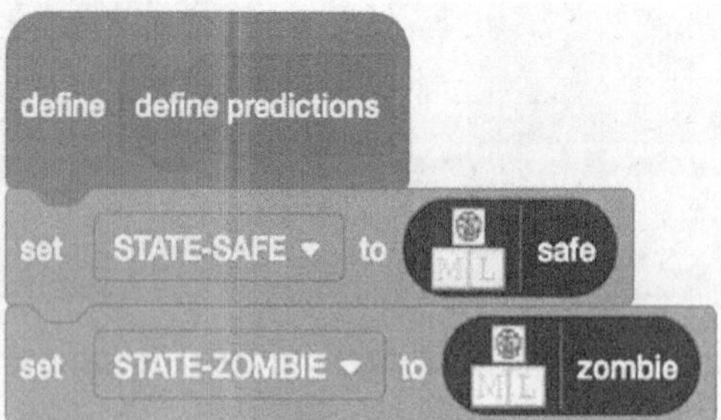

20. In case, If you choose the lighting type sensor, find the define lighting types script, and drag the blocks with the names you gave for the multiple- choice options for lighting types.

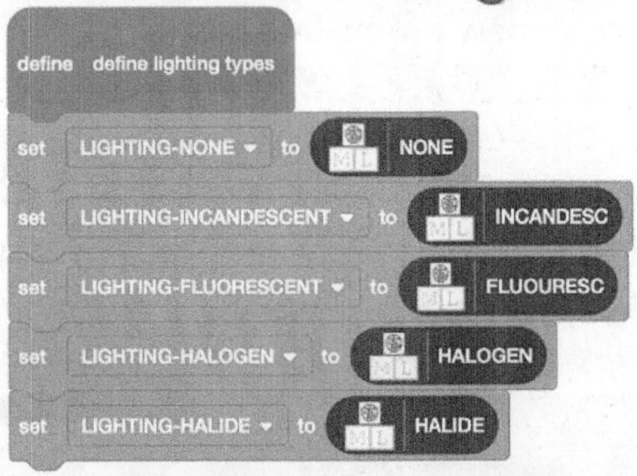

21. If you chose the wall colour sensor, find the define colour names script, and drag in the blocks with the names you gave for the multiple- choice options for colours.

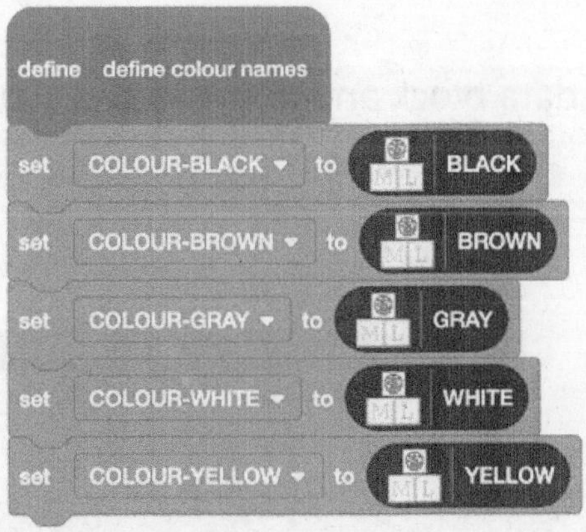

22. If you chose the flooring types sensor, find the define floor types script, and drag in the blocks with the names you gave for the multiple- choice options for flooring.

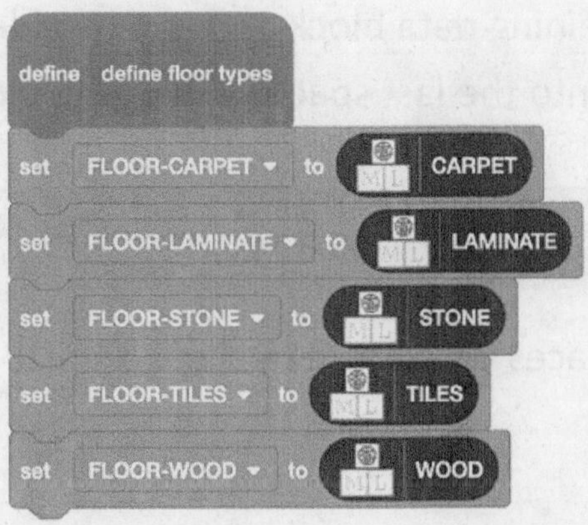

23. Find the when I receive new-rooms-info block.

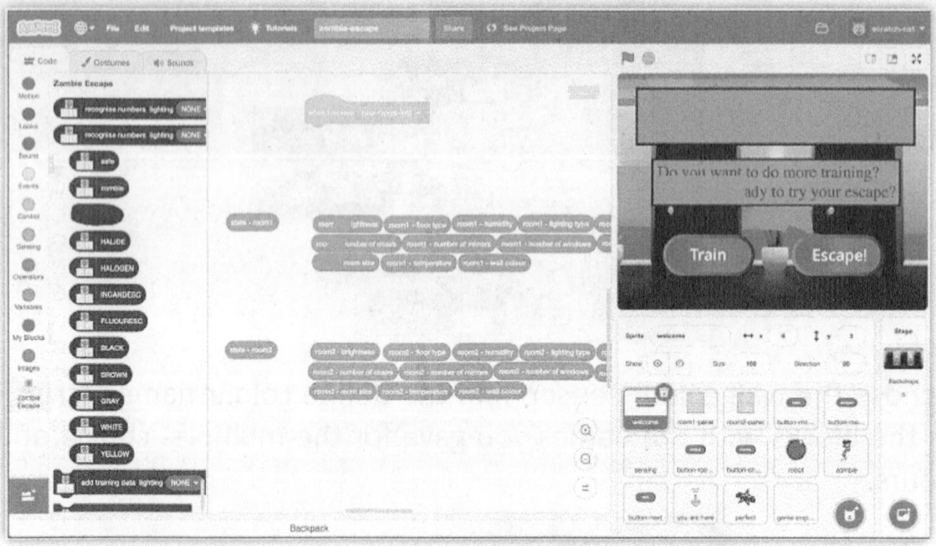

24. Drag an add training data block and add it to the event.

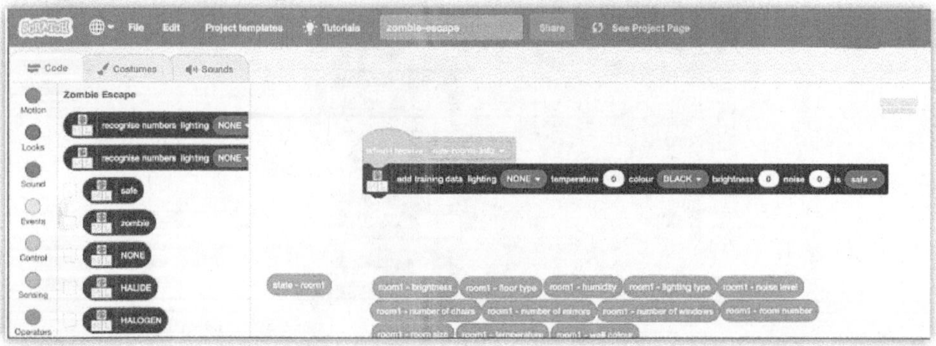

25. Drag state – room1 into the last space on the block
26. Fill the rest of the spaces in the block with room1 values.
27. Drag another add training data block and add it underneath.

    Drag state – room2 into the last space in this new block.

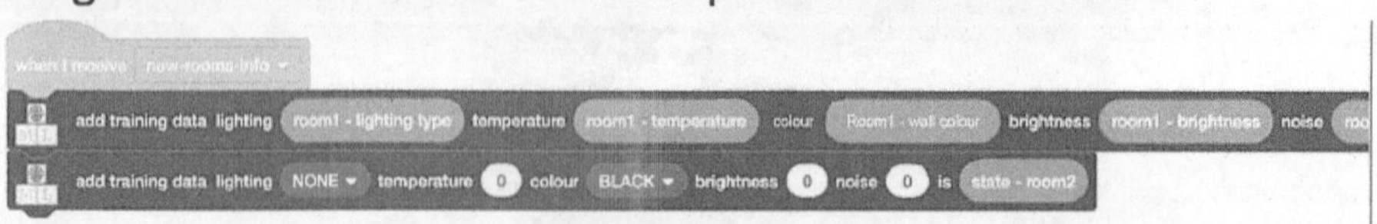

28. Fill the rest of the spaces with room2 values, similar to before.

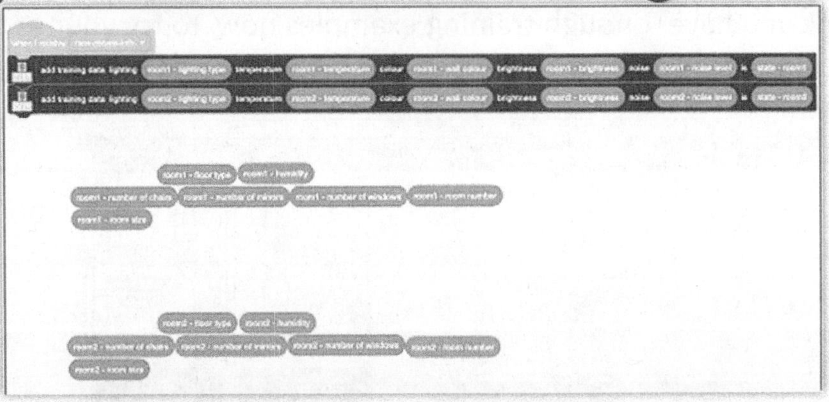

29. Click on the Green Flag and then click Train.

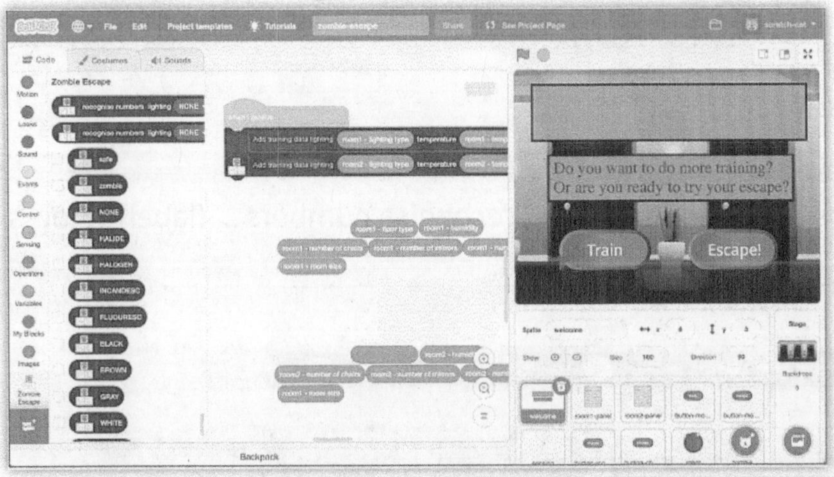

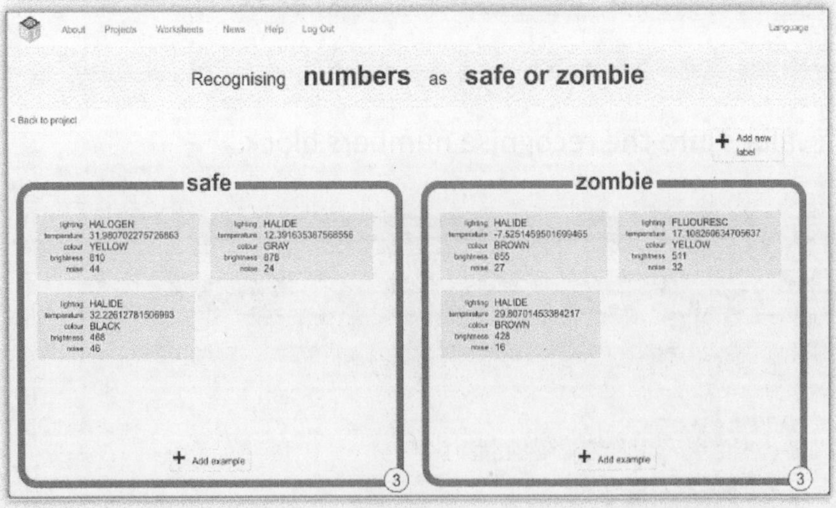

As the robot reaches new rooms, script will add these experiences to the robot's training data.

30. When you think you have enough training examples now, to try your escape, go back to your project Code for the welcome sprite and find the next group of blocks below.

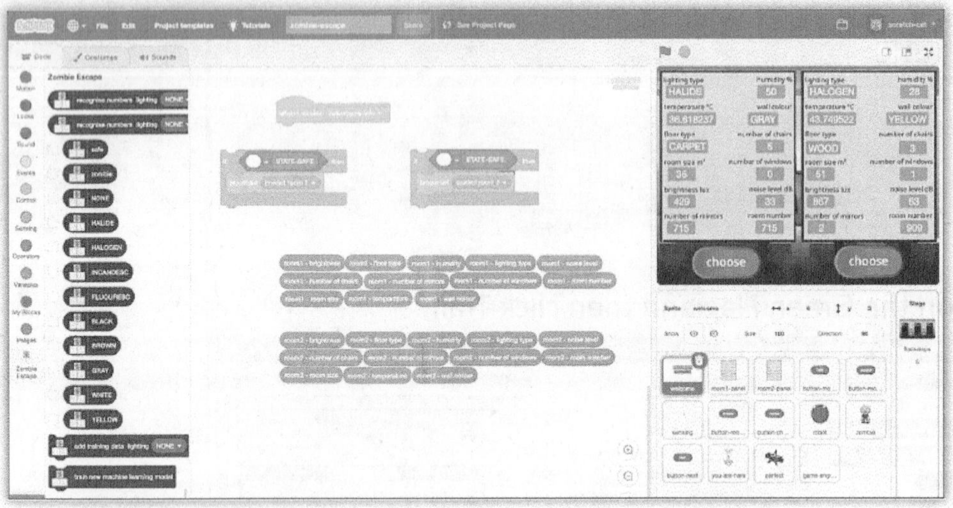

31. Join the groups together, then drag "recognise numbers ... (label)" blocks into the spaces.

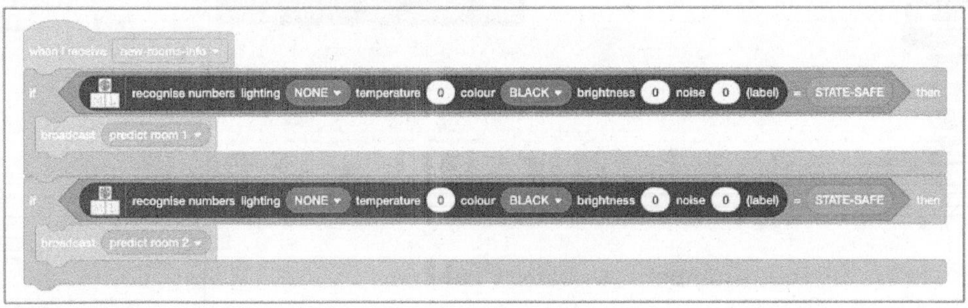

32. Copy the room values into the recognise numbers block.

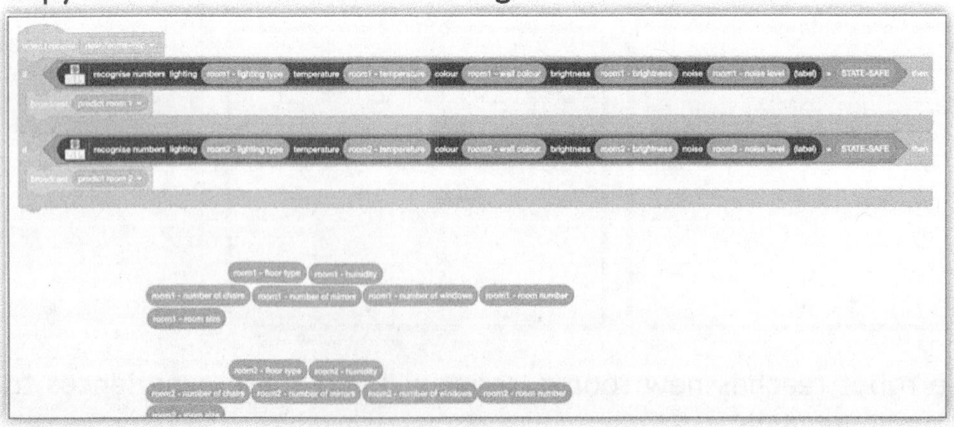

33. Create this final new script.

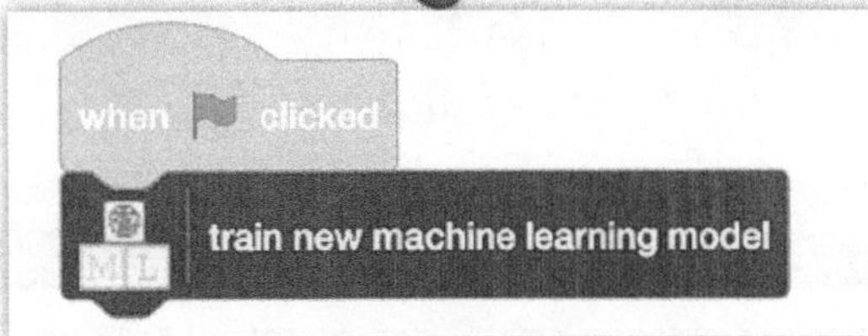

34. Again, Click on the full-screen and Green Flag buttons again, then click on the **Escape!** Button in the project.
35. Machine learning model will use what it has learned to predict which room should be safe.

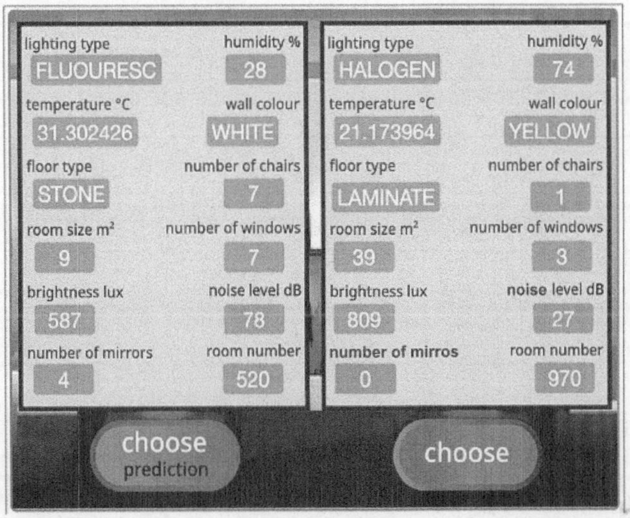

36. When you escape the hotel, the project will display the number of times you were attacked by zombies.

Notes

Sample Paper

Sample Paper

Time: 2 hours **Marks: 50**

A. Multiple choice questions. **1x10=10**

1. Artificial intelligence (AI) is an intelligence which is demonstrated by:
   a. Machines ☐ b. Paper ☐
   c. Human ☐ d. Animals ☐
2. A quip in____ Theorem says "AI is whatever hasn't been done yet."
   a. Tesla's ☐ b. Task's ☐
   c. Tesler's ☐ d. Tailor's ☐
3. AI is artificial life-forms which surpass human intelligence, or it may be a ____________processing technology.
   a. Information ☐ b. Data ☐
   c. Facts ☐ d. Machine ☐
4. To go from point A to B, by using Public transport, you will employ:
   a. Search problem ☐
   b. Planning problem ☐
   c. Search and Planning problem ☐
   d. None of the above ☐
5. To formalize a planning problem, we have to use the concepts of:
   a. State space ☐ b. Transitions ☐
   c. Costs ☐ d. All of the above ☐
6. AI is as old as computer science. Long before we had computers, people thought of the possibility of automatic ________and intelligence.
   a. Questioning ☐ b. Reasoning ☐
   c. Technology ☐ d. None of the above ☐
7. Alan Turing designed a very simple device which can compute anything which is computable and the device is known as:
   a. Turing machine ☐ b. Turning machine ☐
   c. Turn machine ☐ d. Tuen machine ☐

8. AI is meant to be a ________of human intelligence.

a. Similar ☐ b. solution ☐

c. simulation ☐ d. situation ☐

9. Computer process millions of within a second by following the commands given by ______and return the result.

a. Machine ☐ b. Human ☐

c. Pets ☐ d. Animals ☐

10. In Machine learning we work on:

a. Information ☐ b. Data ☐

c. Facts ☐ d. Figures ☐

B. Fill in the blanks. **1×10=10**

1. Self-driving cars works on AI technique such as Search and Planning, Computer vision and _____________.
2. ________, recommends content on Facebook, Twitter, Instagram, and other social media content.
3. AI is used to generate or alter _______content.
4. To solve games using AI, the concept of a ______ is introduced.
5. The different states of the game are represented by________.
6. Artificial Intelligence is when a computer program or machine has the ability to think and_________.
7. In real world instead of perfect information, there is a host of unknown possibilities from missing _________to deliberate deception.
8. To make your computer do the task is known as________.
9. In Machine learning the property of data points is________.
10. Machine learning algorithms are smart algorithms which gives you the power of taking ______on the basis of experience.

C. State whether the following statements are True or False. **1/2×10=5**

1. AI is "cool things that computers can't do.
2. In Teachable machine you cannot train a computer to recognize your images, sounds, & poses.

3. The popularity of AI in the media is because people have started using the term AI when they refer to things which are called by other names.
4. A self-driving car needs to use a variety of sensors.
5. Sophia is a realistic humanoid robot which is capable of displaying human-like expressions and interacting with people.
6. AI creates an opportunity which do not bridge the gap between virtual and physical sales channels.
7. Simplest form to express Bayes rule is in terms of odds.
8. The area of machine learning is divided in subareas according to the kinds of problems being attacked.
9. A neural network can mean either a "real" biological neural network.
10. Wire that transmits the outgoing signal is called an Axon.

D. Match the following. **1/2×10=5**

Column A	Column B
1. Artificial intelligence	i. State space
2. Magic SketchPad	ii. Outcome may be decided only at the end of the game
3. AI in agriculture	iii. Principled way of calculating a conditional probability
4. Bayes Theorem	iv. No labels or correct outputs
5. Set of possible situations	v. Improve crop yield
6. Possible moves between one state to another	vi. Answers are given in the form of yes/no
7. Time/Money required to complete the task	vii. Uses machine learning algorithm
8. Supervised learning	viii. Cost
9. Unsupervised learning	ix. simulation of human intelligence in the machines
10. Reinforcement learning	x. Transitions

E. Answer the following questions. **(2×10=20)**

1. Define the term Machine Learning.

____

2. Write any two applications of Machine Learning.

3. What do you mean by the term Deep Learning?

4. What does Data Science include?

5. Define Turing machine.

6. Explain the idea of John McCarthy about the element of intelligence.

7. Explain how nodes are arranged in Game Tree.

8. Define the term Synapses.

9. What effects the working of Machine learning.

10. Explain how AI is making a difference in day to day life.

GLOSSARY

Artificial intelligence (AI): Intelligence which is demonstrated by machines.

AI Ethics:

- The study of values.
- Generating moral values for good or bad, right or wrong.

Chatbots: Software application which is used to conduct an on-line chat conversation via text or text-to-speech, in lieu of providing direct contact with a live human agent.

Data science: Includes machine learning, statistics, and certain aspects of computer science including algorithms, data storage, and web application development

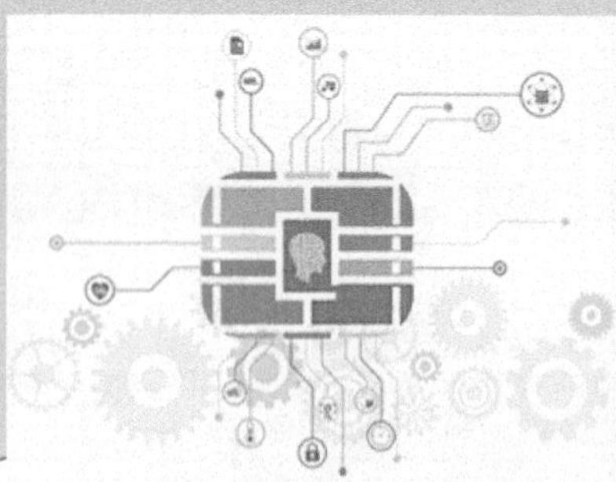

Deep Learning: Machine learning technique which learns features and tasks directly from data. The data can be images, text files or sound.

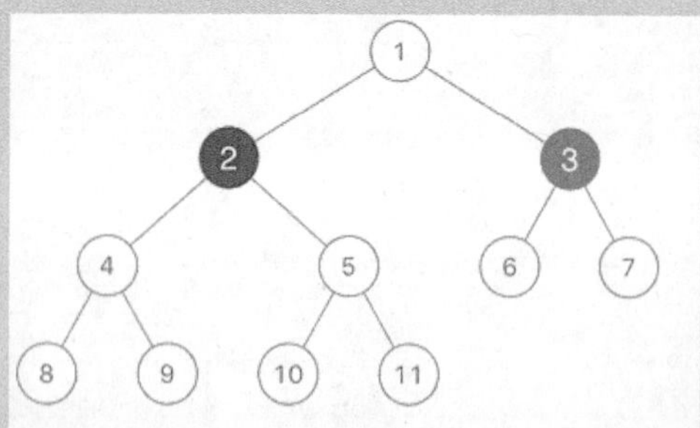

Game tree: Directed graph whose nodes are positions in a game and whose edges are moves.

Machine Learning: Branch of artificial intelligence which is based on the idea that systems can learn from data, identify the patterns and make decisions with minimal human intervention.

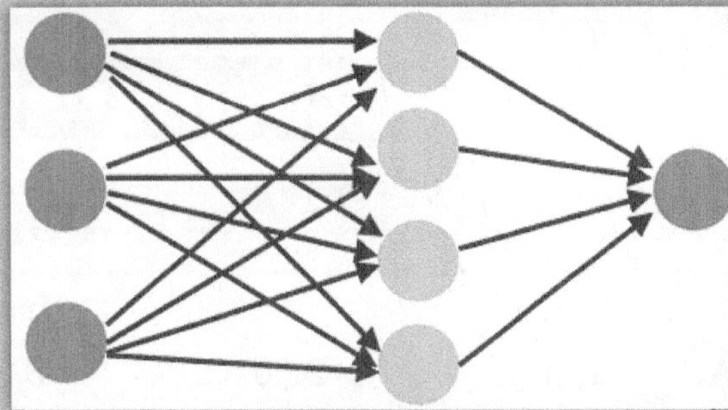

Neural network: Network or circuit of neurons, or in a modern sense, an artificial neural network, composed of artificial neurons or nodes.

Speech Recognition: Subfield of computer science and computational linguistics which develops methodologies and technologies that enable the recognition and translation of spoken language into text by computers

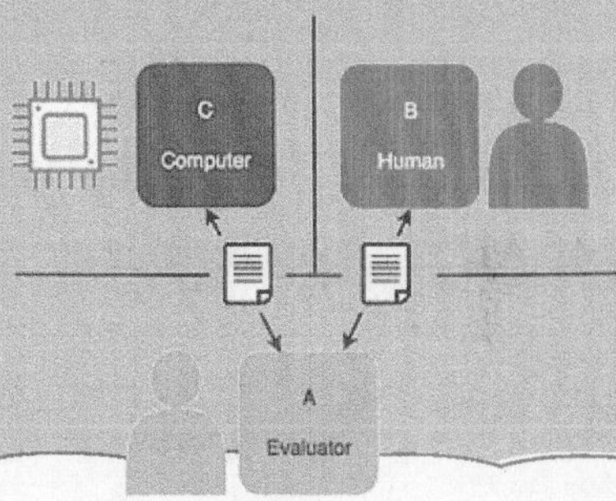

Turing test: AI does not mean to make a computer smart just by knowing more information. AI is to build a machine that can act as if it were smart and seem more human.

Robot: Machine which is programmed by a computer, which is capable of carrying out a complex series of actions automatically.

Robot ethics: Morality of how human's constructs, design, use and treat robots and other artificially intelligent created beings.

Chapterwise Answers

Chapter 1

Brain Bot

A.	1. a	2. d	3. c	4. b	5. a
B.	1. Artificial Intelligence	2. subfield	3. Machine learning		
	4. recognition	5. user			
C.	1. v	2. iii	3. i	4. ii	5. iv

Worksheet

A.	1. True	2. False	3. True	4. False	5. True
B.	1. simulate	2. John McCarthy		3. human intelligence	
	4. AI	5. voice			

Quiz Card

1. c	2. d	3. c	4. a	5. c
6. a	7. c	8. d	9. a	10. a

Chapter 2

Brain Bot

A.	1. a	2. b	3. c	4. d	5. a
B.	1. Puzzle	2. Old	3. computable	4. broken	5. search
C.	1. iii	2. iv	3. i	4. ii	5. iv

Worksheet

A.	1. True	2. True	3. False	4. True	5. False
B.	1. planning	2. information	3. many	4. native Bayes	5. objects

Quiz Card

1. b	2. c	3. d	4. a	5. b
6. a	7. a	8. b	9. c	10. d

Chapter 3

Brain Bot

A.	1. a	2. a	3. b	4. c	5. b
B.	1. problems	2. yes/no	3. labels	4. data	5. games
C.	1. iv	2. i	3. v	4. ii	5. iii

Worksheet

A.	1. True	2. False	3. True	4. True	5. True
B.	1. AI	2. trends	3. surrounded	4. decisions	5. bias

Quiz Card

1. d	2. a	3. a	4. b	5. a
6. b	7. b	8. d	9. a	10. d

Sample Paper

A.	1. a	2. c	3. b	4. c	5. b
	6. a	7. c	8. b	9. b	10. a
B.	1. Decision making		2. Content recommendation		3. visual
	4. game tree		5. nodes	6. learn	7. information
	8. Machine Learning		9. features	10. decision	
C.	1. True	2. False	3. True	4. True	5. True
	6. False	7. True	8. True	9. True	10. True
D.	1. ix	2. vii	3. v	4. iii	5. i
	6. x	7. viii	8. vi	9. iv	10. ii

E.

1. Machine Learning is a subfield of AI, and AI itself is a subfield of computer science. Machine learning enables systems to improve their performance in a given task with more and more experience or data.

2. **Applications of Machine Learning are:**
   - **Speech Recognition:** While using Google, you get an option of "Search by voice," it comes under speech recognition. It converts voice instructions into text.
   - **Traffic prediction:** Predicting the traffic conditions such as whether traffic is cleared, slow-moving, or heavily congested.

3. Deep learning is a subfield of machine learning, and it is the complexity of a mathematical model.

4. Data science includes machine learning and statistics, certain aspects of computer science including algorithms, data storage, and web application development.

5. Alan Turing designed a very simple device which can compute anything which is computable and the device is known as the Turing machine. Machine lead Turing to the invention of programmable computers that can be used to carry out different tasks depending on what they were programmed to do.

6. According to John McCarthy any element of intelligence can be broken down into small steps so that each of the steps is simple and "mechanical" that it can be written down as a computer program.

7. In the game tree, the nodes are arranged in levels that correspond to each player's turns in the game so that the "root" node of the tree is the beginning position in the game.

8. Each axon are connected to one or more dendrites at intersections that are called synapses.

9. Poor data representation affects the working of machine learning.

10. As a consequence of focusing on practicality rather than the big problems, we live our life surrounded by AI; the music we listen to, the products we buy online, the movies and series we watch, our routes of transportation, and even the news and information that we have available, are all influenced more and more by AI.

Notes

Notes